CLEVELAND TRIVIA Quiz Book

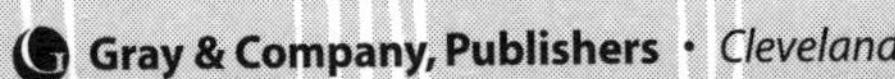

Gray & Company, Publishers · *Cleveland*

© 1996 by Gray & Company, Publishers

Gray & Company, Publishers
1588 E. 40th St.
Cleveland, OH 44103
(216) 431-2665
info@grayco.com

Library of Congress Cataloging-in-Publication Data
Cleveland trivia quiz book / [contributors, Lisa B. Beller ... et al.].
1. Cleveland (Ohio)--Miscellanea. I. Beller, Lisa B.
F499.C64C58 1996
977.1'32--dc20   96-25255

ISBN 1-886228-05-1

Printed in the United States of America

10 9 8 7 6 5 4 3 2 1

The Contributors

Lisa B. Beller (*Geography*) is a freelance writer from downtown Cleveland who prides herself on knowing the city like the back of her hand. She is also Associate Editor of *The Downtown Tab*.

Christopher Johnston (*History and General Editor*) has been a freelance writer since 1988. He has written for many local, regional, and national publications. An history buff since childhood, he has recently edited several books for Frederick C. Crawford and Gray & Company.

Michael DeGrandis (*Sports*) is a partner at Kirtland Capital Partners in Willoughby Hills. A graduate of St. Ignatius High School and Miami (OH) University, he lives in Solon with his wife, Chris, and their two sons, Michael and George.

Barbara Mooney (*Business*) has written about advertising, retailing, small business, and environmental issues for *Crain's Cleveland Business* since 1985. She lives in Cleveland with her husband, writer and editor Eric Broder.

Michael R. Morgenstern (*All*) is an associate editor for Gray & Company, Publishers. He holds a B.A. in History from Purdue and an M.A. in History from Case Western Reserve University. He served as the Besse Fellow assistant editor for the *Encyclopedia of Cleveland History* from 1991 to 1996. He lives in Lakewood with his wife Margaret.

George Muhoray (*Sports*), a graduate of St. Ignatius High School and Miami (OH) University, lives in Bay Village with his three children, Eric, Max, and Alexandra. He can be heard on "The Sports Professionals", a monthly broadcast on WHK 1420 AM.

Jill Sell (*Arts and Entertainment*) is a veteran freelance writer, columnist, and poet whose work has appeared in many local, national and international publications. She has received a number of awards for her arts and entertainment coverage.

Acknowledgements

The contributors would like to acknowledge the assistance of the following people:

Patrice Aylward, Van Dorn Demag Corp.

Molly Beck, The Cleveland Cinematheque

Andre Bernier, meteorologist, WJW TV8

Barbara W. Billings, Western Reserve Historical Society

Eric Broder, Free Times

Nancy Burringshaw, Cleveland Public Theatre

Barbara Caskey, University Hospitals of Cleveland

Cuyahoga Valley National Recreation Area visitor information center

Munroe Copper, Sculptural Engineering, Inc.

Karen Ferguson, Cleveland Museum of Art

Eileen Garne, Pierre's Ice Cream

Chris Hobbs

Joanne Draus Klein, Sun Newspapers

Michael F. Kolman and Michael B. Murphy, Case Western Reserve University

Cheryl Kushner, The Plain Dealer

Les Levine, WHK 1420 AM

Heather Mackey, Cleveland Center for Contemporary Art

Brian McBride, Yellow Cab Co.

Mary McBride

Peg Neeson, WVIZ TV25

Charles Piotrowski, Western Reserve Historical Society

Jane Scott, The Plain Dealer

Anne Sindelar, Western Reserve Historical Society

Sarah Jean Snock and the editors of the Encyclopedia of Cleveland History

The staff of Crain's Cleveland Business

Mary Strassmeyer, The Plain Dealer

Jim Szymanski, WGAR FM 99.5

Gary Thomas, Ohio City Pasta

Susan Walters, KeKA

Rosalie Wieder, copyeditor

James M. Wood, writer

Greg T. Wooten, Thomas/Thomas Antiques

Jonathan Wayne, photographer

Marc Wyse, Wyse Advertising

CLEVELAND TRIVIA Quiz Book

CATEGORIES

AE Arts & Entertainment

B Business

G Geography

H History

S Sports

Answers are found on the
page following the question.

AE Who came first, "The Ghoul" or "Ghoulardi"?

B Industrial forklifts are still generically called by what former Cleveland manufacturer's name?

G On how many interstates can you drive within the Cleveland city limits?

H What Cleveland mayor, who also served terms as governor of Ohio and U.S. senator from Ohio, first made his reputation as a judge fighting organized crime and shutting down several gambling houses?

S Who made the last out at Cleveland Municipal Stadium?

AE Ghoulardi was the first of the two ghoulish late-night movie hosts.

B Towmotor.

G Five: 90; 77; 71; 480; 490.

H Frank Lausche.

S Indians infielder Mark Lewis.

Q

AE Why was the Cleveland Public Theatre originally named Theatre 55?

B What major Cleveland corporation was born in 1911 as Torbensen Gear & Axle Co.?

G Cleveland's metropolitan area population is the largest in the state. True or false?

H Minstrels, fake spiritualists, lecturers, and opera singers entertained at what Superior Ave. theater from 1840–1880?

S What women's golf great did 19-year-old Mary McMillan upset in the finals of the Western amateur golf tournament held in Cleveland in 1946?

AE It was originally intended to be built in the WHK auditorium on E. 55th St.

B Eaton Corp.

G True (at 2,759,000).

H The Globe Theater.

S Mildred (Babe) Didrickson Zaharias.

AE What group of musical freelancers is the official pit band for the Cleveland Ballet and Cleveland Opera?

B What Cleveland publication debuted, as a weekly, on Jan. 7, 1842?

G What 57-story office tower, built on Public Square in 1991, surpassed the Terminal Tower as down-town's (and Ohio's) tallest building?

H How did the corner of W. 25th St. and Detroit Ave. become a vacant lot in 1975?

S After winning the 1945 NFL Championship, the Cleveland franchise moved to what city?

AE The Ohio Chamber Orchestra.

B *The Plain Dealer*.

G Society Center.

H In the explosion that killed underworld denizen Alex "Shondor" Birns, who was blown up in his car while parked in front of Christy's Lounge on that corner.

S The Cleveland Rams moved to Los Angeles.

AE What Cleveland native won an Obie Award in 1964 for her first play, *Funnyhouse of a Negro*?

B Name the restaurant, located on the 38th floor of the Tower at Erieview, that ended 30 years of "high"-class fine dining when it closed in January 1995.

G What main West Side thoroughfare has at different times been known as Sugar Ridge, Coe Ridge, and State St., until its official designation as State Rt. 10 in 1934?

H Long since erased by freeway construction, the area well known as Cleveland's "immigrant ghetto" was at the intersection of Woodland and what street?

S In the 1964 NFL Championship Game, how many touchdowns did wide receiver Gary Collins score in the Browns' winning effort?

A

AE Adrienne Kennedy.

B Top of the Town Restaurant.

G Lorain Rd., in Fairview Park and North Olmsted.

H Broadway.

S Three, all in the second half.

AE Name at least two Pablo Picasso paintings on display at the Cleveland Museum of Art.

B Ten-O-Six is what Lakewood cosmetics company's leading product?

G Which microbrewery is located on Center St. in the Flats?

H On July 23, 1968, what neighborhood of the city became the location of a volatile confrontation between Cleveland police and an African-American militant group that left seven people dead?

S What longtime NHL All-Star also played goalie for the WHA Cleveland Crusaders?

A&E *Woman with Cape; The Artist's Sister (Lola); La Vie; Harem; The Bull's Skull; Fruit, Pitcher and Still Life with Biscuits; Harlequin with Violin; Bottle, Glass, and Fork; Fan, Salt Box, Melon.*

B Bonne Bell.

G The Crooked River Brewing Co.

H Glenville.

S Gerry Cheevers.

AE What Cleveland TV station was the first in Ohio to begin broadcasting?

B Before the Great Depression, Kinney & Levan Co. was a retailer of what? A) men's shoes; B) home furnishings; C) women's hats; D) house linens.

G Name the familiar Italian import store and delicatessen that has been located at 6610 Euclid Ave. since 1912.

H What Cleveland industrialist and philanthropist is credited with introducing golf to Cleveland by founding the Cleveland Golf Club in Glenville in 1895?

S Which Indian made the first regular season hit at Jacobs Field?

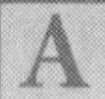

AE WEWS TV5 first went on the air on December 17, 1947.

B B) home furnishings.

G Galluci's (Gust Galluci Co.).

H Samuel Mather.

S Sandy Alomar. He singled in the eighth inning, breaking Seattle Mariners pitcher Randy Johnson's bid for a no-hitter.

AE Ronald Penfound dressed in railroad overalls and cap to appear as what children's TV show character?

B What northeastern Ohio–based conglomerate began with the purchase of "Automatic" Sprinkler Corp. of America in 1963?

G Name the powerful stream emptying into the Cuyahoga River in Valley View whose gorges were recognized as National Natural Landmarks in 1968.

H What kind of photograph was taken for the first time in the U. S. by Dayton C. Miller at Case School of Applied Science in 1896?

S What player did the Browns receive as a result of Bernie Kosar's departure from the team in 1993?

AE Captain Penny.

B Figgie International.

G Tinker's Creek (named for Capt. Joseph Tinker, one of Moses Cleaveland's surveyors).

H An x-ray photograph (of lab assistant Dudley Wick's hand).

S None. Kosar was unconditionally released.

AE What small Brooklyn amusement park, opened in 1951, features a mini-roller coaster, merry-go-round, and pony carts?

B Solon's Cap Toys is the maker of what unusually resilient and flexible male doll?

G W. 117th St. is also referred to by what name?

H For 15 cents admission, what 1880s vaudeville establishment in the Flats offered bowling, concerts, billiards, and a shooting gallery?

S Which Cavalier holds the all-time highest team season scoring average, 24.5 ppg? A) Austin Carr 1973-74; B) Mike Mitchell 1980-81; C) World B. Free 1982-83; D) Ron Harper 1987-88; E) Mark Price 1989-90.

A

AE Memphis Kiddie Park.

B "Stretch Armstrong."

G Memphis Ave.

H The White Elephant.

S B) Mike Mitchell.

AE What location was originally slated for the controversial Claes Oldenburg sculpture, "Free Stamp"?

B Cleveland's Claud H. Foster (1872-1965), known as the "Doctor of Car Riding," invented two of the most basic of standard automobile features. Name one.

G What insects regularly invade Cleveland's lakeside neighborhoods and suburbs around the end of May and the first week of June each year?

H What Cleveland restaurateur and primary owner of Chef Hector's restaurant at 823 Prospect was deemed "the world's greatest chef" by Benito Mussolini?

S Professional hockey returned to Cleveland in 1992 when the Lumberjacks moved here from what city?

AE Public Square, in front of the BP America Building.

B Shock absorbers and automatic windshield wipers.

G The non-biting but bothersome "Canadian soldiers," also known as may flies or midges.

H Hector Boiardi (Chef Boy-ar-dee).

S Muskegon, Michigan.

AE What was the inaugural event at Gund Arena?

B Although he could not play it, Walter Holtkamp was internationally known for his construction and installation of what instrument?

G Every March, the buzzards return to Hinckley. But technically, they're not buzzards. What is the proper name for these birds?

H Indian chief, Native American rights activist, president of the Preservative Cleaner Co., and longtime Cleveland resident until his death in 1950, Oghema Niagara (1865-1950) was more popularly known by what name?

S Name the renowned golf course architect who designed the Blue and White courses at Fowler's Mill Golf Club in Chesterland.

AE A concert by Billy Joel.

B The organ. (Holtkamp organs can be found at St. John's Cathedral, Baldwin-Wallace College, CWRU, Oberlin, MIT, Yale, and the Air Force Academy.)

G Turkey vultures.

H Chief Thunderwater.

S Pete Dye.

AE What longtime Cleveland newspaper columnist had a brief stint as anchor man on WKYC TV3 in 1993?

B What did the Leece-Neville Co. develop here in Cleveland? A) steel furnaces; B) automotive alternators; C) arc welders; D) bolt and lock sets.

G Which East Side suburb was formerly the location of a religious colony?

H Who was Carl Stokes's nemesis on Cleveland City Council during his two-term administration?

S Who won the 1979 US Amateur Golf Championship held at Canterbury Golf Club?

AE Dick Feagler.

B B) automotive alternators.

G Shaker Heights. (It was the site of the North Union Shaker Community, which settled in the area in 1822, but ceased to exist in 1889.)

H James Stanton, Head of Council.

S Mark O'Meara.

AE Philanthropist Jane Kirkham's fund-raising efforts and vision helped save what Cleveland arts institution?

B Who was Cleveland's self-professed "Diamond Man" from the mid-1960s through the 1980s?

G What public housing development on Woodland Ave. was built on land formerly occupied by the popular amusement resort Luna Park?

H Why were fences placed around each of the four quadrants of Public Square in 1839?

S In 1980, two spectators were injured during what famous Ted Stepien promotional stunt?

AE   The Playhouse Square theater district.

B   Larry Robinson.

G   Woodhill Homes.

H   To keep out livestock.

S   The dropping of softballs from the Terminal Tower's 52nd floor.

AE Name the Euclid Ave. watering hole where club scenes for the film *Light of Day* were filmed.

B What restaurant featuring a pink flamingo mascot rated two visits from President Bill Clinton?

G What divides Cleveland's East Side from its West Side?

H What did delicatessen operator and Tribe fan Charlie Lupica do for 177 days during the 1949 baseball season?

S What Indians player is the only major leaguer ever to hit home runs from both sides of the plate in the same inning?

AE The Euclid Tavern, in University Circle.

B Parma Pierogies.

G Public Square. (Streets are numbered to the east and west of Ontario St., which cuts through the square.)

H He sat atop a flagpole. (For his efforts, he received a personal invitation from owner Bill Veeck to be carried aloft into a game.)

S Carlos Baerga.

AE What color were the sports pages of the old *Cleveland News*?

B A friendly yellow duck serves as a mascot for what northeast Ohio tape maker?

G Lime St. was once home to what type of utility facility in 1893?

H Originally opened in 1856 as the Cleveland Homeopathic Hospital, it is considered Cleveland's oldest private hospital. Name it.

S Opening Day 1975 marked the first time a major league baseball team was coached by a black manager. Who was he?

AE Pink.

B Manco Inc.

G An electric power plant.

H Huron Rd. Hospital, now known as Meridia Huron Hospital.

S Frank Robinson, Tribe manager from 1975 to 1977.

AE Santa's "keeper of the keys" spent more than 30 Christmas seasons on Halle's seventh floor and had his own holiday TV show. Name him.

B In September 1992, the *Free Times* assumed the role of Cleveland's primary alternative weekly. What previous tabloid did it replicate in both style and substance?

G The former Fairhill Blvd. was renamed in the 1990s for what pair of Cleveland politicians?

H What national conflict sparked the fiery birth of Cleveland's Industrial Revolution, predominantly in steel mills and petroleum refineries in the Flats?

S Tulane University abolished its basketball program following a point-shaving scandal in the 1980s. What future Cavalier, who was cleared of all charges, played for its last team?

A

AE Mr. Jing-a-ling (Earl Keyes).

B *The Cleveland Edition* (published from 1984 to 1992).

G Louis and Carl Stokes.

H The Civil War.

S John "Hot Rod" Williams.

Q

AE Whom did Dorothy Fuldheim kick off her TV show for swearing and using a defamatory pork reference regarding police?

B In 1973, Randall Park Mall was erected by the Edward J. DeBartolo Corp. on the site of what former race track?

G Name Cleveland's most populous suburb, with more than 100,000 residents.

H If you had traveled through the Flats by canal boat in 1826, you might have been tempted to stop and see the orangutan, fire eaters, and Siamese twins on display at what newly opened establishment?

S The Cavaliers are the first Cleveland franchise in the NBA. True or false?

AE   Sixties radical Jerry Rubin.

B   Randall Park Race Track.

G   Parma (incorporated as a city in 1931).

H   The Stage House (later renamed Franklin House).

S   False. In 1946-47, the Cleveland Rebels were a charter member of the Basketball Association of America, later renamed the NBA.

AE The Cleveland Orchestra's first concert was held in 1918 at an arsenal still standing on Bolivar Rd. Name it.

B What prestigious Cleveland automaker ran out of gas in 1931 after a 42-year ride?

G What natural watershed was the notorious discovery site for many of the Torso Murder victims?

H What Cleveland monument has sculptures depicting members of the infantry, artillery, cavalry, and navy?

S Who did Muhammad Ali fight at the Richfield Coliseum on March 24, 1975?

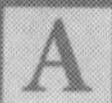

AE Grays Armory.

B Peerless Motor Car Co.

G Kingsbury Run, named for early settler James Kingsbury (1767-1847).

H The Soldiers and Sailors Monument (dedicated July 4, 1894).

S Chuck Wepner.

AE What children's theater is the oldest of its kind in Greater Cleveland?

B What division of Riser Foods Inc. was named after the St. Lawrence Seaway?

G What local publication is known as "Ohio's Black Newspaper"?

H This legendary football coach and trophy name-sake, born and raised in Ohio City, was christened Johann Wilhelm. Name him.

S There are three pairs of brothers of which one played for the Browns and the other for the Indians. Name them.

AE Heights Youth Theatre.

B Seaway Foods.

G The Call and Post.

H John W. Heisman (1869-1936).

S Karl Pagel, 1B, Indians (1981-83) and Mike Pagel, QB, Browns (1986-91); Alex Johnson, OF, Indians (1972) and Ron Johnson, RB, Browns (1969); Pat Kelly, OF, Indians (1981) and Leroy Kelly, RB, Browns (1964-73).

AE What are the call letters of Cleveland's internationally recognized classical music radio station?

B Today, you're more likely to encounter a doorman than a bouncer at the site of the old Mowrey's Tavern. What first-class establishment now occupies that location?

G The Terminal Tower was built over what? A) sacred burial ground; B) quicksand; C) 100 years ago; D) red clay.

H Which Cleveland mayor's wife was unable to attend a White House dinner because it was her bowling night?

S In 1955, who was the East Tech and Baldwin-Wallace track grad who won the Sullivan Award, bestowed upon the best amateur athlete in the nation?

AE WCLV.

B Renaissance Cleveland Hotel.

G B) quicksand.

H Ralph J. Perk's wife, Lucille.

S Harrison "Bones" Dillard.

AE This Cleveland artist, who died in 1995, created statues of Winston Churchill, Jesse Owens, and George Washington, and a limestone grizzly bear now situated at the Cleveland Museum of Natural History. Who is he?

B What former downtown department store is remembered for its annual multi-story Christmas tree display?

G What is the only full-scale, suburban-style grocery store in the downtown area?

H The southwest corner of Case Ave. (now E. 40th St.) and Euclid Ave. was once home to what great industrialist?

S Though Otto Graham's number 14 has been retired by the Browns, what other number did he wear for many years as QB?

AE William McVey.

B Sterling-Lindner Co.

G Dave's Supermarket, at E. 33rd St. and Payne Ave.

H John D. Rockefeller.

S 60.

Q

AE What was the title of the Michael Stanley Band's live album?

B Sam Foti Sr. founded what Euclid flexible hose maker in 1982?

G The Society Tower on Public Square is how many feet taller than the Terminal Tower?

H What type of stone was used to build the Old Stone Church?

S During the late 1970s and early 1980s, what two Browns running backs shared the same backfield and the same last name, but were not related?

A

AE *Stage Pass*.

B Hose Master Inc.

G 240.

H Berea sandstone.

S Mike and Greg Pruitt.

Q

AE What Lakewood native led a swing band whose slogan began, "Swing and Sway with …"?

B Who was the first director of the Gateway Economic Development Corp.?

G What designation is given to any local tree that is thought to have been in existence since the time of the city's founding in 1796?

H Ed Nishnic provided key information that saved the life of his father-in-law, alleged Nazi war criminal John Demjanjuk, by helping to overturn Demjanuk's earlier conviction in what court?

S *Doonesbury* character B.D. is based on what former St. Ignatius High School quarterback?

AE Sammy Kaye.

B Tom Chema.

G It is called a "Moses Cleaveland Tree."

H The Israeli Supreme Court.

S Brian Dowling (who also starred at Yale during creator Gary Trudeau's college years).

AE What was the name of Barnaby's invisible parrot?

B What popular news magazine was published in Cleveland between 1925 and 1927 in order to get it to the West Coast faster?

G Name downtown's only ice-cream stand.

H Which NASA space shuttle astronaut grew up in Willoughby?

S By what name was Michael Russell, Cavs forward (1974–79 and 1983–85) better known?

AE   Long John.

B   *Time Magazine.*

G   Apple Cart (at E. 43rd & Superior).

H   Greg Harbaugh.

S   Campy Russell.

AE What method does the Fine Arts Association use at its Willoughby School of Fine Arts to teach violin and piano to four-year-olds?

B Where did the first Arabica coffee shop open?

G What shape is Shaker Square?

H What was the original name of John Carroll University?

S Located on Brookpark Rd., this bowling alley, featuring 78 lanes, is the largest in Ohio. Name it.

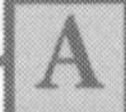

AE The Suzuki method.

B On Coventry Rd. in Cleveland Hts.

G Octagonal. Architects changed the design from a circle to an octagon to accommodate more automobiles.

H St. Ignatius College. (It was originally located at the current site of St. Ignatius High School in Ohio City.)

S Stardust Lanes.

AE The Gerald E. Brookins Museum of Electric Railways in Olmsted Township displays more than 30 electric interurban trains and streetcars. By what name is it more popularly known?

B Lobster Newburg was the favorite frozen dinner of what Cleveland frozen foods pioneer?

G At the beginning of the 20th century, what percentage of Clevelanders were foreign-born? A) 20; B) 33; C) 40; D) over 50.

H What type of "doctor" was William Avery Rockefeller, father of John D.?

S Who was the last Indians pitcher to lead the AL in wins?

AE Trolleyville, USA.

B Vernon Stouffer.

G B) 33 percent.

H A "botanic physician" or itinerant dispenser of cure-alls.

S Gaylord Perry, who won 24 games in 1972.

AE   What husband-and-wife comedy team of stage and radio fame were married in Cleveland while performing in Playhouse Square?

B   What Cleveland company's mustard has been served at League Park, Cleveland Stadium, and now Jacobs Field—since 1930?

G   In 1906, numerical designations were substituted for the names of Cleveland streets running in what direction?

H   Which was the first Cleveland bank: A) Commercial Bank of Lake Erie; B) Central National Bank; C) National City Bank

S   During the 1994 season, why was Albert Belle suspended for seven games?

A

AE George Burns and Gracie Allen.

B Joe Bertman Foods, Inc., producer of Ball Park Mustard.

G North-south.

H A) Commercial Bank of Lake Erie.

S Belle was found to be using a corked bat.

AE What Euclid Ave. coffeehouse and former bowling alley started as a folk venue but became the city's most influential rock-n-roll club before closing in 1969?

B The Powerhouse, now the centerpiece of the Nautica complex in the Flats, was originally built by Marcus A. Hanna to provide power for what?

G What Kirtland institution is home to more than 4,800 different plants, making it the largest of its kind in the U.S.?

H World War I prevented construction of what facility at the north end of the Mall that would have completed the Group Plan?

S With almost 40 years on the job, what Benedictine coach has the most wins of any Cleveland high school football coach?

A

AE La Cave.

B Streetcars.

G Holden Arboretum.

H A railroad station.

S Augie Bossu.

AE What riverfront establishment opened in 1987 in a former sugar warehouse, becoming the first part of the Nautica complex?

B What was the nickname of John Davey, the father of tree surgery and founder of the Davey Tree Expert Co. in Kent?

G What East Side suburb, originally incorporated as Euclidville in 1917, received its current name in a high school contest in 1920?

H Which U.S. President traveled to Cleveland to attend the prize social event of 1903, the marriage of Ruth Hanna (Marcus's daughter) and Medill McCormick?

S In 1987, the Indians experienced the "*Sports Illustrated* curse" when two of its players appeared on the cover that predicted Cleveland to be the year's best team. The Indians, along with what two cover-boys, went on to lose 100 games?

AE Shooter's Restaurant.

B "The Tree Doctor."

G Lyndhurst. (The name was taken from Lyndhurst, New Jersey.)

H Theodore Roosevelt.

S Cory Snyder and Joe Carter.

AE Founded in 1915, Karamu House is the oldest interracial metropolitan center for the arts in the United States. What does its name mean?

B What was the original name of *Industry Week*, the Cleveland-based national business weekly?

G What is the name of W. 100th St.?

H Who designed the geodesic dome that covers the American Society of Metals' Materials Park in Russell?

S Where did Cleveland Barons owner Nick Mileti move the team in 1973?

A

AE "Karamu" is Swahili for "a place of joyful meeting."

B *Steel*.

G West Blvd.

H R. Buckminster Fuller.

S Jacksonville, Florida.

AE Name the rock band that recorded their album, *Short Bus*, in a rented house next door to Great Northern Mall.

B In 1851, Isaac Hewitt and Henry Tuttle founded what Cleveland iron ore company?

G Where is the only remaining covered bridge in Cuyahoga County?

H When it opened in 1963, this local two-year community college set a national record with an initial enrollment of 3,039 full- and part-time students. Name it.

S In 1946, who was quoted in the *New York Times* as saying, "It's not that I love Cleveland less, but that I love Los Angeles more."?

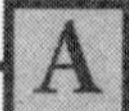

AE   Filter.

B   Oglebay Norton Co.

G   Strongsville, near Valley Parkway in the Cleveland Metroparks Rocky River Reservation.

H   Cuyahoga Community College.

S   Cleveland Rams owner Dan Reeves, before moving the team to Los Angeles.

AE What popular Cleveland night spot has moved from Cornell Ave. to E. 24th St. and then to E. 53rd and Euclid Ave. since opening in 1967?

B What house of cards was built by Jacob Sapirstein?

G What eight-story building, once affiliated with Warner Brothers, sits on the southeast corner of Payne Ave. and E. 21st St.?

H Who of the following is not buried at Lake View Cemetery? A) Marcus A. Hanna; B) Charles F. Brush; C) Henry A. Sherwin; D) Joc-o-sot; E) Alexander Winton.

S In 1984-85, what two Browns running backs rushed for 1,000 yards each?

AE The Cleveland Agora.

B American Greetings Corp.

G The Film Building.

H D) Joc-O-Sot; he is buried in Erie Street Cemetery.

S Earnest Byner and Kevin Mack.

AE What annual community college event has featured entertainers Ella Fitzgerald, Miles Davis, Count Basie, Dizzy Gillespie, and Sarah Vaughn?

B Name downtown's only authentic boxcar diner.

G The heart of Cleveland's Chinatown is at the convergence of which two downtown streets?

H What type of mill did Holsey Gates and his brothers operate on the Chagrin River that eventually gave its name to the eastern suburb Gates Mills?

S In 1970, Browns All-Star Paul Warfield was traded to the Miami Dolphins in exchange for what player?

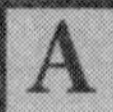

AE The Tri-C (Cuyahoga Community College) Jazz Fest.

B Ruthie and Moe's, at E. 40th and Payne Ave.

G E. 30th and Payne Ave.

H A sawmill.

S For the rights to draft Purdue quarterback and All-American Mike Phipps.

AE Who hosted "Mad Theater I and II", Saturday afternoons on WUAB TV43?

B From 1954 to 1973, what prominent downtown property was a Hilton Hotel?

G Name the two bowling alleys located downtown.

H Moses Cleaveland and his surveying party were representatives of what organization?

S Name at least one of the professional Cleveland baseball teams that preceded the Indians.

AE "Super Host" Marty Sullivan, who also served briefly as producer and the station's voice-over man.

B The Statler Office Tower at E. 12th and Euclid Ave.

G Ambassador Lanes and Twin Lanes.

H The Connecticut Land Co.

S The Forest Citys (1871-84), Spiders (1887-99), Blues (1900-04), Naps (1905-14).

AE What popular annual Cleveland Museum of Art show first opened in the spring of 1919, allowing each artist to enter 10 items for display?

B What is Cleveland's only raw material export?

G What union's headquarters are located at E. 22nd and Carnegie Ave.?

H Approximately how many buildings were razed to make way for construction of the Terminal Tower on Public Square: A) 1; B) 30; C) 350; D) more than 1,000?

S Who was the last Indian to hit for the cycle?

AE The May Show.

B Salt. (By Akzo Nobel Salt, on Whiskey Island.)

G The Cleveland Federation of Musicians (housed in the Musicians Union building).

H D) more than 1,000

S Andre Thornton, April 22, 1978 versus the Boston Red Sox.

AE What Euclid facility, formerly a school, now houses the Cleveland-Style Polka Hall of Fame?

B CSU law professors Jane Picker and Lizabeth Moody founded what law firm that limited its practice to sexual discrimination cases—a first in 1972?

G What was the former name of the section of I-77 running between downtown and Independence?

H On September 25, 1872, "60 or 70 of the most companionable and cultured gentlemen" of Cleveland formed what club?

S In the 1987 AFC Championship Game against Denver, which Browns player made "The Fumble"?

AE   Shore Cultural Centre.

B   Women's Law Fund Inc.

G   The Willow Freeway. (It was officially incorporated into the federal interstate system upon its completion in 1973.)

H   The Union Club.

S   Earnest Byner.

AE Joan Baez, Pete Seeger, and Ritchie Havens are all past headliners at what northeast Ohio folkfest?

B What slogan encircles a logo of the Terminal Tower on the sides of Yellow and Zone taxicabs?

G Prior to World War II, Cleveland's Central Avenue district housed the city's largest population of which ethnic group? A) Ukranian; B) African-American; C) Asian; D) German.

H Who was the first African-American elected to Congress from Ohio?

S What artist created the updated version of Chief Wahoo for the Cleveland Indians in 1947?

AE The Cuyahoga Valley Heritage Festival.

B "I Like Cleveland."

G B) African-American.

H Rep. Louis Stokes, who began serving the 21st district in 1968.

S Walter Goldbach.

AE Name the literary organization founded in 1975 by Cleveland poets Cyril A. Dostal and Chris Franke.

B The Cleveland Provision Co. was, for almost 100 years, Cleveland's leading what? A) grocery store; B) meat packing company; C) dry goods store; D) cannery.

G The summer estate of John D. Rockefeller encompassed some 700 acres on Cleveland's East Side, and included 18 miles of roadways and trails, a lake, a horse-trotting course, and a nine-hole golf course. What was its name?

H What position did John Hay hold in President Lincoln's administration?

S What East Tech graduate went on to win four gold medals in the Berlin Olympics of 1936?

AE   The Poets' League of Cleveland.

B   B) Meat packing company.

G   Forest Hill.

H   Private secretary.

S   Jesse Owens.

AE What was the first published poem of (James) Langston Hughes, who began his writing career while attending Central High School in Cleveland?

B This restaurant, opened in 1893 on Sheriff St. (E. 4th), has a long and venerable history as the select dining spot of Cleveland's theater crowd, catering to both performers and theater patrons. Name it.

G In 1920, Cleveland's Jewish population was thickly clustered in the vicinity of what two streets?

H The sixth Catholic Bishop of Cleveland (1945-66) established 47 elementary schools and 12 high schools, and also remodeled St. John Cathedral and St. John College. What was his name?

S Name these Indians: Sudden Sam; Rapid Robert; Large Lenny.

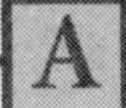

AE "The Negro Speaks of Rivers," published by the NAACP publication, *Crisis*, in 1921.

B Otto Moser's Tavern.

G Woodland Ave. and E. 55th St.

H Archbishop Edward Francis Hoban.

S Sam McDowell, Robert Feller, Len Barker.

AE Name the two founders of the School of Cleveland Ballet who were responsible for its transformation into the Cleveland Ballet in 1976?

B What bustling shopping area at the intersection of Lorain Rd. and Rocky River Dr. is named for a 19th-century grocer and postmaster?

G Euclid Ave. at E. 105th St. was known as what district in the 1920s? A) Uptown; B) Midtown; C) Central; C) Downtown.

H Which former Cleveland mayor worked as a broadcaster for television station WNBC in New York?

S Who was the first free agent signed by the Indians to a multi-million-dollar contract?

AE Dennis Nahat and Ian Horvath.

B Kamm's Corners. (Named for Oswald Kamm, who in the late 1800s walked daily to Rocky River to fetch residents' mail from the Nickel Plate Railroad Station. Mail was marked "Kamm's, Ohio" to indicate its final destination.)

G A) Uptown.

H Carl B. Stokes.

S Wayne Garland, a pitcher, signed for $2.3 million over 10 years in 1976.

AE What Cleveland television personality regularly reminded viewers to "stay sick, turn blue"?

B What company single-handedly created the Berea Quarries in the Rocky River Reservation?

G The highest temperature ever recorded in Cleveland was 104 degrees Fahrenheit in 1988. During which month?

H Myth would have it that this body of water was named for the consternation it caused Cleveland's founding party when they mistook it for the Cuyahoga, but it was really named after a French trader. Name it.

S What former baseball player and Penobscot Indian is the only individual after whom a major league baseball team has been named?

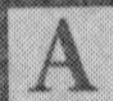

AE "Ghoulardi," aka Ernie Anderson.

B Cleveland Quarries Co.

G June.

H The Chagrin River. (Named after Sieur de Saguin.)

S Louis Francis Sockalexis, legendary namesake of the Cleveland Indians.

AE How many Pulitzer Prizes have been awarded to *The Plain Dealer*?

B In the 1950s, what now-defunct company published *Webster's New World Dictionary* and was the nation's largest bible printer?

G The lowest temperature ever recorded in Cleveland was reached in January, 1994. How low did it go?

H Name the two Cleveland Teamster leaders whose violent tactics and alleged mob ties led to a federal probe of the Union in 1957 and suspension of the Teamsters from the AFL-CIO.

S Who won the 1984 Chevrolet World Championship of Women's Golf at Shaker Heights Country Club?

AE One. (In 1953, to Edward Kuekes for his editorial cartoon, "Aftermath," which addressed the discrepancy between national draft and voting age requirements.)

B World Publishing Co.

G -20 degrees Farenheit.

H William Presser and N. Louis (Babe) Triscaro.

S Nancy Lopez.

AE Where does Archibald Willard's famous painting, *The Spirit of '76*, hang?

B What company rehabilitated the Terminal Tower and the old Halle's department store during the 1980s?

G Market Square Park is located near what market?

H John L. Severance, John D. Rockefeller, Marcus A. Hanna, Samuel Mather, and Langston Hughes graduated from which Cleveland High School?

S What early 1970s Cavalier point guard later went on to coach the team and then became the winningest coach of all time while leading the Atlanta Hawks?

A

AE In Cleveland City Hall.

B Forest City Enterprises.

G The West Side Market.

H Central High School.

S Lenny Wilkens.

AE Which of the following apply to the Cleveland Public Library? A) first open shelves; B) first children's reading room; C) world's largest chess library; D) first 24-hour/7-day-a-week dial-in access to on-line catalog ; E) all of the above.

B What Cleveland auto maker converted its E. 79th St. facilities during World War II to produce scout cars, half tracks, tank destroyers, and personnel carriers?

G Which West Side municipality became the first community in the nation to mandate the use of seatbelts in automobiles, in 1966?

H During the 1880s, "Drew's Dime Museum" in the Flats offered what kind of entertainment?

S Who ended Don Cockroft's 12-year reign as kicker of the Browns in 1981?

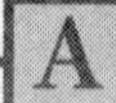

AE   E) all of the above.

B   White Motor Corp.

G   Brooklyn.

H   A freak show.

S   David Jacobs, a free agent from Syracuse.

AE What historic theater near E. 9th St. and Euclid Ave., equipped with four hydraulic stage jacks and a huge water tank for aquatic spectacles, was demolished in 1981 and replaced with a parking facility?

B What Cleveland radio station, now featuring sports-talk, was one of only six stations in the U.S. when it went on the air in 1921?

G This inner-city neighborhood was named for the thick, shady glens through which small streams flowed into Doan Brook. Name it.

H In which Cleveland suburb was the nation's first camp for girls opened in 1895?

S Which two tennis greats played for the Cleveland Nets of the World Team Tennis League?

AE The Hippodrome Theater.

B WHK-AM.

G Glenville (incorporated as a village in 1870 and annexed to the city of Cleveland in 1905).

H Rocky River.

S Martina Navratilova (1976) and Bjorn Borg (1977).

Q

AE "Krocus Bohemeth" was the pen name used by what internationally acclaimed musician when he wrote for *Scene Magazine*?

B Formally incorporated in 1960, this Cleveland-based company specializes in key supplies, prescription eyewear, and engraved gifts, and operates 2,000 retail outlets. Name it.

G Riveridge Township (est. 1926) occupied only 48 acres bounded by the Rocky River and the airport. By the 1980s it was a virtual ghost town, after serving for many years as a large trailer park. In 1992 it was annexed by what city?

H By what name was the Steamer *William G. Mather* affectionately referred to after Mather and his bride Elizabeth Ring Ireland sailed on it after their wedding at Trinity Cathedral in 1929?

S Which longtime Brown offensive lineman became an Ohio state senator?

A

AE David Thomas (founder of Pere Ubu).

B Cole National Corp.

G Fairview Park.

H "The honeymoon ship."

S Dick Schafrath (OT, 1959-71).

AE Which Cleveland dance company, founded in 1982, features members who use wheelchairs?

B Which Cleveland TV station, established in 1985, was one of the Fox Network's first affiliates?

G Cleveland experienced rapid population growth with the completion of what canal in 1832?

H What Cleveland suburb was the birthplace of Archibald M. Willard, painter of the "Spirit of '76"?

S What offensive lineman wore number 66 while serving as Jim Brown's workhorse blocker?

AE Cleveland Ballet Dancing Wheels.

B WOIO.

G The Ohio and Erie Canal.

H Bedford.

S Gene Hickerson (1958-60, 1962-73).

AE What Japanese animated film, directed by Katsu Hiro Ohtomo, has had more screenings than any other film at the Cleveland Cinematheque?

B Which of the "Big Six" accounting firms originated in Cleveland?

G In the early 20th century, where was the "largest dancing pavilion in the world"?

H Name the Dakota Sioux Indian who moved to Cleveland in the late 1960s to unite the Indian community and establish the Cleveland American Indian Center?

S What two locations have the Harold T. Clark Tennis Courts occupied?

AE *Akira* was shown 11 times.

B Ernst & Young.

G Euclid Beach Amusement Park.

H Russell Means.

S Ambler Park in Cleveland Heights and, since 1978, the eastern end of the Municipal parking lot off the Shoreway.

AE Charles "Chuck" Young, director of music operations for KYW-AM in the 1950s and 1960s, was said to have an uncanny ear for picking potential hit songs. Name at least one No. 1 song he helped break.

B Name the labor movement's oldest active newspaper, founded in Cleveland in 1891.

G In 1987, Jeffrey Lundgren and his wife were expelled from the Reorganized Church of Jesus Christ of Latter-Day Saints. The Lundgrens then moved to a nearby farm, where in 1989 they murdered the Avery family. In what town did these grisly events take place?

H Who was known nationally as "the Boy Mayor?"

S Name the pacer that set a new world record on the inaugural day of grand circuit racing at North Randall track in 1909.

A&E "Chantilly Lace," Big Bopper; "Splish Splash," Bobby Darin; "Rockin' Robin," Bobby Day; "Born Too Late," Poni Tails (who were from Lyndhurst).

B *The Cleveland Citizen.*

G Kirtland.

H Dennis Kucinich.

S Uhlan.

AE What 1985 film by Jim Jarmusch was set in Cleveland?

B When it opened in 1988, it became the first operational Cleveland brewery since C. Schmidt closed its plant in 1984. Name it.

G From its inception in 1973, the Woollybear Festival (celebrating the legendary weather-forecasting caterpillar) has grown into Ohio's largest one-day festival. Where is it held each year?

H This set of rules, adopted by Cleveland in 1904, was the first of its kind in the U.S. Within two years, 29 cities had duplicated it. What was it?

S In 1971, what 16-year-old women's tennis phenom defeated Virginia Wade to retain the Whitman Cup for the U.S. at Harold T. Clark Stadium?

AE *Stranger than Paradise.*

B The Great Lakes Brewing Co.

G Vermilion.

H The first comprehensive building code. (It comprised six sections of regulations detailing inspections, permit types, building sizes and sites, fire protection, and elevator construction).

S Chris Evert

Q

AE In 1984, Dorothy Fuldheim conducted her last interview. With whom?

B According to the late great ad slogan, "You go, or _______ pays your tow."

G What eight-story building, located at 812 Huron Rd., was designated a historic landmark structure in 1973?

H Manry Park in Willowick is named for intrepid Cleveland adventurer Robert N. Manry, who achieved what nautical feat?

S In the 1987 NFL college draft, what player did the Browns send to the San Diego Chargers in exchange for the rights to Duke linebacker Mike Junkin?

AE President Ronald Reagan.

B Sohio (Standard Oil Co.'s trade name).

G The Caxton Building.

H He sailed the Atlantic Ocean alone.

S Linebacker Chip Banks.

AE What Cleveland native is called "America's Polka King"?

B Cyrus Eaton and William G. Mather established this company in 1930. At the time of its merger with LTV, it was the fifth-largest steel producer in the U.S. Name it.

G What street was known as "The Buffalo Road" in the early- to mid-19th century?

H The Central Market area was known by what name prior to 1950?

S Name the Indians fan who has been beating a drum in the bleachers for more than 20 years.

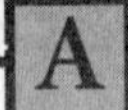

AE   Frankie Yankovic.

B   Republic Steel Corp.

G   Euclid Ave.

H   Sheriff Street Market.

S   John Adams.

AE What famous Cleveland figure was the victim of a bomb blast on March 24, 1970?

B Cleveland's largest business organization is best known by its acronym, COSE. What does that acronym stand for?

G This bridge over the Cuyahoga was renamed the Harold H. Burton Memorial Bridge in 1986. By what name is it still more commonly known?

H Name two of the first four settlers who arrived in 1797 with their families.

S What St. Joseph High School standout played collegiate basketball at Ohio State and pro ball with the Indiana Pacers, and is a commentator for CBS?

AE "The Thinker," sculptor August Rodin's renowned figure of a seated man, located outside of the Cleveland Museum of Art.

B Council of Smaller Enterprises.

G The Main Avenue Bridge. (The bridge was erected in 1938-39, during Burton's tenure as mayor of Cleveland.)

H Lorenzo Carter, Elijah Gun, Ezekiel Hawley, and James Kingsbury.

S "Special K" Clark Kellogg.

AE What famous comedian and pianist made his operatic conducting debut with "The Magic Flute" for Cleveland Opera in 1976?

B What brewing company, which made its home in Cleveland and operated from 1907 to 1952, was best known for its "Black Forest" beer?

G From 1930 to 1940, four suburbs experienced a growth rate of more than 500 percent. Name at least two.

H Amos Spafford and Seth Pease created Cleveland's first two … what?

S Where was the illuminated statue of Chief Wahoo relocated after the Cleveland Indians moved out of Municipal Stadium?

AE Victor Borge.

B Cleveland Home Brewing Co.

G Cleveland Heights, Shaker Heights, Garfield Heights, Parma.

H Maps.

S The Reinberger Gallery at the Western Reserve Historical Society.

AE What film's cast featured the 1948 Cleveland Indians?

B In 1911, the U.S. Supreme Court ruled that this trust, operated out of Cleveland, was a monopoly and forced its dissolution. Name it.

G Which West Side suburb is home to the historic "Oldest Stone House" and the Nicholson House?

H President Benjamin Harrison, ex-President Rutherford B. Hayes, General William Tecumseh Sherman, Chief Justice Melville Fuller, and Congressman (and future President) William McKinley attended what local event on Decoration (Memorial) Day, 1890?

S What Collinwood and Cleveland State grad fulfilled his childhood dream of starting at shortstop with the Indians in the early 1980s?

AE *The Kid from Cleveland.*

B The Standard Oil Trust.

G Lakewood.

H The dedication of President James A. Garfield's tomb at Lake View Cemetery.

S Jerry Dybzinski.

AE The old science and business annex to the Cleveland Public Library, razed in 1994 to make way for a new science annex, was the former home to what Cleveland newspaper?

B What local civic planning organization is comprised of the CEOs of the 50 largest local companies?

G What racetrack begins in Summit County, briefly runs through Cuyahoga County, and ends back in Summit County?

H At the stroke of noon on June 26, 1936, what famous American pushed a button to open Cleveland's Great Lakes Exposition?

S What was bowler Steve Nagy's claim to fame in 1955?

AE *The Plain Dealer*.

B Cleveland Tomorrow.

G Northfield Park. (The northern quarter of the track, encompassing turns three and four, lies in Cuyahoga County.)

H President Franklin D. Roosevelt.

S He became the city's first national match game champion.

AE This co-founder and first conductor of the Cleveland Orchestra went on to become the first national director of the WPA's Federal Music Project from 1935 to 1937. Who was he?

B What national labor organization has its Local 1 in Cleveland?

G Now reconditioned for hikers and bicyclists, what antique transportation corridor winds it way through the Cuyahoga Valley National Recreation Area?

H Whose credo was "Make no small plans"?

S What are the names and numbers of the four Cavaliers whose jersey numbers are retired?

AE Nikolai Sokoloff (1886-1965).

B The American Newspaper Guild. It earned the "Local 1" designation by predating the national organization by four months.

G The Ohio & Erie Canal towpath.

H Daniel Burnham (architect, city planner, and father of Cleveland's Group Plan of 1903).

S Austin Carr (34), Bingo Smith (7), Larry Nance (22), Nate Thurmond (42).

AE   Children's TV show host Captain Penny reminded young viewers at the end of each show: "You can fool some of the people all of the time, all of the people some of the time, but you can't fool …" whom?

B   What Cleveland printing company, still in operation under its founder's name, was started with his soldier's wages from the Civil War?

G   Busted by Eliot Ness in the 1930s, the notorious Harvard Club casino once flourished in which Cleveland suburb?

H   A single fountain is all that remains of philanthropist John L. Severance's elegant Longwood estate, which was demolished to build what shopping mall?

S   Held on July 3, 1931, what was the first major sporting event at Cleveland Municipal Stadium?

A

AE Mom.

B S. P. Mount Printing Co.

G Newburgh Heights.

H Severance Center, in Cleveland Heights.

S A heavyweight boxing championship between Max Schmeling and William "Young" Stribling.

AE What local 1960s TV variety show became so popular that it was taped and syndicated nation-wide (it later relocated to Philadelphia)?

B William O. Walker published and wrote for what Cleveland newspaper?

G What all-night eatery is located at W. 51st St. and Detroit?

H In December of 1978, what ignominious honor befell the city of Cleveland?

S In the 1970 All-Star Game, Indians catcher Ray Fosse was injured for the season in a home plate collision with what National League player?

AE "The Mike Douglas Show."

B *The Call and Post*.

G The Big Egg.

H It became the first major American city to default on its financial obligations since the Depression.

S Cincinnati Red Pete Rose.

AE Built in 1896 at 4939 Broadway, this structure was the first hall in Cleveland to be owned by a nationality group. What is it?

B Scott S. Cowen was appointed as the first dean of what area business school?

G The Shaker Lakes, now designated as a National Environmental Educational Landmark, were created by the 19th-century damming of what body of water?

H For whom was Baldwin-Wallace College in Berea named?

S Which Indians fielder was most responsible for halting Joe DiMaggio's 56-game hitting streak?

A

AE The Bohemian National Hall.

B The Weatherhead School of Management at Case Western Reserve University.

G Doan Brook.

H John Baldwin and James Wallace.

S Third baseman Ken Keltner, who made two fine defensive plays to help halt the streak.

AE What was the first evening-length story ballet performed by Cleveland Ballet?

B Heart surgeon Dr. Floyd Loop succeeded William Kiser as CEO of what large Cleveland employer in 1989?

G This building, erected on Public Square in the 1890s, was the first in Cleveland to feature a complete structural steel frame and was notable for its arched terra cotta entranceway. It was razed in 1982 to make way for the Sohio (BP America) Building. Name it.

H This former mayor of Cleveland went on to become a U.S. senator and associate justice of the U.S. Supreme Court, where he was instrumental in decisions outlawing segregation in railroad cars and public schools. Name him.

S American Arthur Ashe and German Christian Kunke achieved what distinction at Harold T. Clark Stadium in 1970?

AE *The Nutcracker*, first performed by the troupe in 1981.

B The Cleveland Clinic.

G The Cuyahoga Building. (The terra cotta entrance-way was dismantled and reassembled as part of the Library of the Western Reserve Historical Society.)

H Harold H. Burton, mayor of Cleveland 1935-40, senator 1940-45, and Supreme Court justice 1945-58.

S They recorded the longest singles match in Davis Cup history.

AE All the members of the musical group founded in 1935 by Cleveland Orchestra violinist Hyman Schandler had what in common?

B What is the former name of Meridia Euclid Hospital?

G Home to the Front Row Theater from 1974 to 1993, this municipality was also the first community in Cuyahoga County to require underground wiring and ornamental street lighting in all new subdivisions. Name it.

H The Cleveland Chapter of the League of Women Voters sponsored a debate between which two U.S. Presidential candidates?

S Who was the Browns' quarterback prior to Frank Ryan?

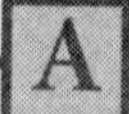

AE They were all women. (The group was The Cleveland Women's Orchestra).

B Parkwood Hospital.

G Highland Heights.

H Jimmy Carter and Ronald Reagan. It was held on October 28, 1980, in the Music Hall.

S Milt Plum (1957-61).

AE During the Cleveland Play House's 1992 International Theater Exchange, this play was performed entirely in Russian. Name it.

B The first national convention of what business service organization was held in Cleveland on May 18, 1916?

G What is the most commonly accepted meaning of the word "Cuyahoga"?

H In what year was the National Air Show first held at Burke Lakefront Airport?

S Who hit his 500th career home run at League Park on August 11, 1929?

AE   Tennessee Williams's *A Streetcar Named Desire.*

B   The Kiwanis Club. (At that convention, the 16 clubs then in existence developed the idea of forming an international organization.)

G   "Crooked river" or "Crooked water" (although "Place of the jawbone" or "Crooked like a jawbone" are also accepted translations).

H   1964.

S   Babe Ruth.

AE Who has had the longest tenure as director of the Cleveland Museum of Art?

B Joe DiMaggio pitched what Cleveland-made product?

G Cleveland has been named an "All-America City" more times than any city in the nation. How many times?

H Cleveland's airport is named after William Rowland Hopkins. What job did he hold from 1924 to 1929?

S Who is the last native Clevelander to win one of the four "major" golf tournaments on the PGA tour?

AE William M. Milliken (director from 1930 to 1958).

B The Mr. Coffee automatic coffeemaker (developed by North American Systems in 1971).

G Five; in 1949, 1982, 1984, 1986, and 1993.

H City Manager. (During his tenure, he obtained the land adjacent to Brookpark Rd. upon which Cleveland Municipal Airport was built.)

S Tom Weiskopf, who won the British Open at Troon, Scotland, in 1973.

AE Edris Eckhardt, the Cleveland-born sculptor, glassmaker, and teacher, revived a method of fusing gold between sheets of glass to produce the first gold glass in 2,000 years. In what land was such glass last produced?

B The Telling-Belle Vernon Co. was the first business in Cleveland to deliver what beverage in glass bottles?

G This East Side stream empties into Lake Erie at Bratenahl, where Samuel Mather built his summer home, Shoreby, on its banks. Name it.

H What Cleveland singer-actress and civic philanthropist served as an alternate delegate to the United Nations during the Eisenhower Administration?

S Although the Browns traded for the rights to Syracuse All-American Ernie Davis in 1961, he never played for them. Why not?

A

AE Egypt.

B Milk.

G Nine Mile Creek.

H Zelma Watson George.

S Davis was diagnosed with leukemia prior to the 1962 season.

AE What were the two most famous roles of Cleveland native and Play House alumna Margaret Hamilton?

B What is the parent company of the Care Bears, Holly Hobbie, and Strawberry Shortcake?

G During its construction in the 1930s, this roadway was among the largest WPA projects in the country. Name it.

H Where did The Slovak League for U.S. Slovaks meet with the Bohemian National Alliance for U.S. Czechs on October 22, 1915 to sign a historic agreement calling for the formation of Czechoslovakia?

S Although the Cavs traded for Danny Ferry during the 1989-90 season, he did not play in a Cavaliers' uniform until the 1990-91 season. Where did he play in the interim?

AE The Wicked Witch of the West in *The Wizard of Oz*, and Cora, in a series of Maxwell House TV commercials.

B American Greetings Corp.

G The Memorial Shoreway (initial section), dubbed the Lakefront Highway, running from E. 9th to E. 72nd at Gordon Park.

H The Bohemian National Hall on Broadway.

S Ferry was under contract with Il Messaggero of the Italian League.

AE What book by Cleveland-born author John O'Brien, who committed suicide in 1994, became an Oscar- and Golden Globe-winning film in 1996?

B What Cleveland manufacturer made hydraulic parts for the U.S. air fleet during World War II?

G Where will you find the Cleveland Cultural Gardens?

H John Patterson Green is acknowledged as the first African-American to be elected to political office in Cleveland. What office did he first hold?

S What former voice of the Browns was often heard to exclaim, "5 4 3 2 1 Touchdown"?

AE *Leaving Las Vegas*, for which Nicholas Cage won Best Actor.

B Parker Hannifin Corp.

G In Rockefeller Park, along Martin Luther King, Jr. Blvd near University Circle.

H Justice of the Peace. (He was later elected to both bodies of the Ohio legislature.)

S Nev Chandler.

AE In what city was the Great Lakes Shakespeare Festival held before it moved to the Ohio Theater in 1982?

B Founded in 1845, this is the oldest bank in Cleveland. Name it.

G Annexed to the city of Cleveland in 1910, this village was originally called Collamer and was noted for its fertile soil, ideal for the production of grapes, peaches, and cherries. Name it.

H What petroleum waste product fueled the explosive growth of Rockefeller's Standard Oil Co. in the late 19th century?

S Name these Browns: Glue Fingers; The Toe; Turkey.

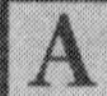

AE Lakewood. The event was sponsored by the Lakewood Board of Education.

B National City Bank.

G Collinwood. (The settlement of Collamer was named for Judge Jacob Collamer, the postmaster general under President Zachary Taylor.)

H Gasoline.

S Dante Lavelli, Lou Groza, Joe Jones.

Q

AE What is the nickname of the former Ford assembly plant on Euclid Ave. at E. 117th, now used by the Cleveland Institute of Art for studios and classrooms?

B Name the company that owns the Finast supermarket chain.

G Where in Cleveland does a rainshower occur at least once every day?

H James F. Lincoln, the head of Lincoln Electric from 1914 until his death in 1965, was vehemently opposed to what Democratic initiative developed during the 1930s?

S Bill Belichick played professional football with the New York Giants before becoming a coach. True or false?

AE "The Factory" (formally known as the McCullough Center).

B First National Supermarkets Inc.

G The Cleveland Metroparks Zoo RainForest.

H The New Deal.

S False. Bill Belichik never played professional football.

AE Name the first modern dance company from Greater Cleveland to perform nationally and internationally.

B What Cleveland newspaper was the first to get its presses rolling, on July 31, 1818?

G Which bank is not at the intersection of E. 9th and Euclid Ave.: A) Huntington; B) National City; C) Bank One; D) Society?

H The Rev. Bruce Klunder died in Glenville protesting the construction of what kind of building (which he maintained promoted segregation)?

S Where is Hi Corbett Field located?

AE The Footpath Dance Co., founded in 1976 by Alice Rubinstein.

B *The Cleaveland Gazette & Commercial Register.*

G C) Bank One.

H An inner-city school. (Klunder was killed in 1964 when a bulldozer at a construction site backed over him.)

S Tucson, AZ (the former spring training home of the Tribe).

AE Name the weekly column written by humorist Eric Broder since 1987, first for *The Edition* and now for *Free Times*.

B Two overlapping Ds on the sleeve of your T-shirt means it came from what local retailer?

G What spectacular weather phenomenon might be spotted offshore when very cool northwest winds blow over Lake Erie's warm summertime water?

H With its statue of Mayor Tom L. Johnson, the northwest quadrant of Public Square has tradition-ally been associated with what essential right of all U.S. citizens?

S Which innovation was not pioneered by Browns namesake and head coach, Paul Brown? A) the use of game films; B) messengering plays with substitutes; C) wind sprints; D) face guards; E) helmet radios; F) play books.

AE "The Great Indoors".

B Daffy Dan's T-shirt shops.

G A waterspout.

H Free speech.

S C) wind sprints.

AE What organization was founded as a community co-op in 1972 to promote and develop the arts in Cleveland and now sponsors the annual "Art in Special Places" festival?

B What Cleveland company sponsored the famous annual "trophy" airplane races around pylons anchored in Lake Erie?

G Mather Manslon is located on the campus of which area university?

H During the 1970s, the county Democratic Party operated under a co-chairmanship of three area politicians: county commissioner Hugh A. Corrigan, former city council president Anthony Garofoli, and Congressman Louis Stokes (later replaced by George Forbes). What was the party's nickname for this arrangement?

S What player stole the first base at Jacobs Field?

AE NOVA (New Organization for the Visual Arts).

B Thompson Products (now TRW).

G Cleveland State University.

H "The Troika."

S Omar Vizquel.

AE What Cleveland native, a former prom queen, cheerleader, and Miss Ohio, had roles in *Jungle Fever*, *Losing Isaiah*, and *The Flintstones*?

B In the late 1980s, Kemper Corp. bought what Cleveland investment house?

G The statue of Moses Cleaveland on Public Square faced north when it was placed there in 1888, but it was moved in the 1980s. Which direction does it face now?

H At its dedication in 1866, what W. 9th St. building, now gone, was billed as the "largest building under one roof in the United States"?

S The Browns were one of the first teams to create a drug intervention and counseling group. What was the name of their group?

A

AE Halle Berry.

B Prescott Ball and Turben.

G East.

H Union Depot.

S The Inner Circle.

AE Who became the first woman in Cleveland to host her own TV show when "Distaff," a cooking show sponsored by Frigidaire, debuted February 14, 1948 on WEWS TV5?

B Name the Cleveland-based law firm that became a legal powerhouse after the 1939 merger of Tolles, Hogsett & Ginn with Day, Young, Veach & Leferer.

G What 4.5-square mile industrial suburb swells in population from about 700 to almost 18,000 each business day?

H Cleveland political giants Marcus A. Hanna and Mayor Tom L. Johnson battled as powerhouses of rival political parties. They also competed in what business?

S Who holds the Cavs record for the most points scored in a game?

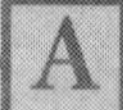

AE Alice Weston.

B Jones, Day, Reavis & Pogue.

G Cuyahoga Heights. (Situated adjacent to the I-77/I-480 interchange, it is home to 175 businesses and industries, including BP America and Reliance Electric.)

H They had competing streetcar lines.

S Walt Wesley, who scored 50 points against the Cincinnati Royals on Feb. 19, 1971.

AE Name the writer and creator of Cleveland detective Milan Jacovich, the sleuth of such mystery novels as *The Cleveland Connection*, *The Duke of Cleveland*, *Deep Shaker*, and *Pepper Pike*.

B Name the first beer produced by the Crooked River Brewing Co.

G Where can you find the world's largest indoor amusement park?

H Central High School was the first public high school west of the Alleghenies. True or false?

S Which Brown returned two punts for touchdowns against the Pittsburgh Steelers on October 24, 1993?

AE Les Roberts

B Settler's Ale.

G At the I-X Center, adjacent to Cleveland Hopkins International Airport.

H True. Established in July 1846, it was controversial because of the prevailing belief that education beyond the elementary level should be private.

S Eric Metcalf.

AE Syndicated radio comedian Howard Stern celebrated reaching #1 on local airwaves ratings in 1995 with a media blitz staged at what Flats location?

B What new product illuminated Nela Park for the first time in 1936?

G What charter boat docks at the E. 9th St. pier?

H A native of Puerto Rico, he became the first Hispanic elected to public office in Ohio when he won a seat on the Cuyahoga County Court of Common Pleas in 1988. Name him.

S Who were the Browns' opponents in the 1970 premiere broadcast of ABC Monday Night Football?

AE Tiffany's parking lot.

B Fluorescent lighting.

G Goodtime III.

H Jose A. Villanueva.

S The New York Jets.

AE This arts and crafts gallery/studio on the grounds of the Metroparks Huntington Reservation plays host to the annual "Renaissance Fayre" on Labor Day weekend. Name it.

B Cleveland confectioner Clarence Crane, father of poet Hart Crane, was also father of what candy?

G What is the western-most stop on the RTA Green Line?

H What publication initially refused to print the Cleveland Electric Illuminating Co.'s advertisements touting "Cleveland ... The Best Location in the Nation" in 1944?

S When Jim Tressel's Youngstown State football team won the NCAA Division 1-AA Championship in 1991, Jim and his father, Lee, became the only father-son team to win national titles. What college did Lee Tressel coach?

AE Baycrafters, in Bay Village, 28795 Lake Rd.

B Life Savers. (As head of the Crane Chocolate Co. in 1912, Crane developed them as an alternative to chocolates, which were messy in the summer and didn't sell well.)

G Tower City / Public Square.

H The New York Times.

S Baldwin-Wallace College.

AE Which Cleveland Orchestra musical director (1971–1982) was known for featuring "Great Composers of Our Time"?

B Baby car seats are a primary product line for what northeast Ohio firm?

G Originally called Lenox, this suburban city is noted for the creation of the first municipally owned bus line, in 1931. Name it.

H On July 5, 1886, Cleveland Councilman Charles Reader arranged for the demolition of what North Union Shaker landmark as a vote-winning scheme?

S Who hit the longest home run at Cleveland Municipal Stadium?

A

AE Lorin Maazel.

B Century Products Inc.

G North Olmsted.

H The gristmill.

S Luke Easter, approximately 477 feet into the upper deck.

Q

AE In 1970, the opening of what pop musical had Mayor Carl Stokes and members of the Cleveland vice squad in attendance at the Hanna Theater?

B Cleveland's oldest engineering firm, once known as the "Stadium Builders for the Nation," designed Cleveland Municipal Stadium, Yankee Stadium, Fenway Park, and the old Comiskey Park. Name it.

G What was the former name of E. 89th St.?

H What Cleveland industrialist helped install new, more durable engine valves in Charles Lindbergh's *Spirit of St. Louis* just hours before its famous flight across the Atlantic?

S What Cleveland Brown was the first black player inducted into the Football Hall of Fame?

AE *Hair.*

B Osborn Engineering Co. (established in 1892).

G Bolton Ave.

H Frederick Coolidge Crawford.

S Browns fullback Marion Motley.

AE Which of these locations was never home to the Cleveland Center for Contemporary Art: A) a Euclid Ave. storefront; B) Bellflower Ave.; C) the Cleveland Museum of Art; D) the Cleveland Play House complex?

B What Cleveland plastics company was once the nation's largest maker of jail cells?

G By what name is the area from W. 3rd to W. 10th streets, bordered by Superior and St. Clair avenues, known?

H Cleveland's oldest building, on Euclid Ave., was at one time a stagecoach stop and is now a museum. Name it.

S In 1958, what injury threatened the career of Indians pitcher Herb Score?

AE C) The Cleveland Museum of Art.

B Van Dorn Demag Corp.

G The Warehouse District.

H Dunham Tavern.

S Score was hit in the eye with a line drive off the bat of New York Yankee Gil McDougal.

AE At which original Flats establishment did patrons once sit at long drinking tables to quaff beer while listening to Dixieland music?

B What beloved local bakery closed its doors in 1992?

G Which downtown street begins at E. 13th and ends at E. 55th?

H On historic Mall A, War Memorial Fountain by sculptor Marshall Fredericks honors 4,000 Clevelanders who died in which two wars?

S In 1960, what Western Reserve University student won the gold medal in free skating at the Winter Olympics in Squaw Valley, California.

A

AE Fagan's.

B Hough Bakeries Inc.

G Payne Ave.

H World War II and the Korean War.

S Dave Jenkins.

AE Late night TV movie hosts Chuck Schodowski and John Rinaldi are better known by what nicknames?

B What company is the title sponsor of Cleveland's premier marathon and 10-K run?

G W. 6th St. was formerly known by what name?

H When elected to the Municipal Court of Cleveland in 1923, she became the first elected female municipal judge in the United States, remaining on the bench until 1959. Name her.

S In 1988, what player did the Browns receive from the Washington Redskins in exchange for Earnest Byner?

AE   "Big Chuck and Little John".

B   Revco D.S. Inc.

G   Bank St.

H   Mary B. Grossman (1879-1977).

S   Mike Oliphant.

AE In 1982, artistic director James Levine used his connections as a criminal lawyer to get local motorcycle gangs to help build what Cleveland theater?

B Cleveland's floating maritime museum, The Steamship William G. Mather, was once the flagship for what company?

G The Old Erie Street Bookstore is located on what street?

H Which downtown building was designed by Henry Bacon, the architect for the Lincoln Memorial in Washington, D.C.?

S What basketball powerhouse did CSU defeat in the first round of the 1986 NCAA tournament?

A

AE The Cleveland Public Theatre.

B Cleveland-Cliffs Iron Co.

G E. 9th.

H The Halle Building.

S Indiana University.

AE James Hutchkiss Rogers, a *Plain Dealer* music critic, teacher, and composer, wrote more than 50 compositions for what instrument?

B What Elyria company is an international leader in wheelchair manufacturing?

G W. 25th St. and Pearl Rd. A) Intersect at I-71; B) run parallel to each other; C) are the same street; D) run perpendicular to each other.

H Under whose mayoral administration was Burke Lakefront Airport, the first downtown airport in the U.S., built?

S Who has been the radio voice of the Cavs for all but two years of their existence?

A

AE The organ.

B Invacare.

G C) are the same street.

H Thomas A. Burke.

S Joe Tait.

AE What Lyndhurst-raised singer/songwriter and former Raspberry began classical musical training at the Cleveland Institute of Music at the age of two?

B Noted for its remarkable efficiency during World War II, this precision airplane parts company grew from 56 employees in 1940 to 8,700 in 1944. It is now known as Lucas Aerospace Power Equipment Corp. Name it.

G Cleveland's eastern suburbs receive more snow as a result of what weather phenomenon?

H What doctor and co-founder of the Cleveland Clinic Foundation had a U.S. Army hospital in Parma named in his honor? (The hospital was housed in a building that is now part of the Cuyahoga Community College campus.)

S In 1920, Bill Wambsganss of the Indians became the only player ever to do what in World Series history?

AE   Eric Carmen.

B   Jack & Heintz Co.

G   The "lake effect."

H   Dr. George Washington Crile, Sr. (1864-1943). (Crile, who received many medical honors, is acknowledged as having performed the first successful blood transfusion, in 1905.)

S   He completed an unassisted triple play, against the Brooklyn Dodgers.

AE What was the name of the afternoon TV program hosted by Dorothy Fuldheim and DJ Bill Gordon?

B Who purchased the Chesapeake & Ohio Railroad in the 1920s, creating a towering"need for a new terminal in downtown Cleveland?

G Which interstate is also known as the Berea-Airport Freeway?

H During the War of 1812, what was located next to the Lakeside Courthouse at Lakeside and W. 3rd St.?

S Which Cavalier made a layup in the wrong basket during a game against Portland in the Cavs' first season as an expansion team?

AE "The One O'Clock Club."

B Oris Paxton and Mantis James Van Sweringen.

G I-71.

H A fort and army supply depot.

S John Warren.

AE What was considered Cleveland's premier rock music radio station in the 1960s?

B An explosion at the Thor Manufacturing Co. in 1903 helped convince Cleveland's lawmakers to prohibit the sale of what product five years later?

G What transit system is the only one in Ohio still using electric trolley cars?

H The area in the Flats below St. Malachi's church and W. 25th St. was once known by what name, owing to its large Irish population?

S Tragedy struck the Indians family when which two pitchers died in a boating accident during 1993 spring training?

A

- **AE** WHK-AM.
- **B** Fireworks.
- **G** The RTA's Shaker Rapid Transit.
- **H** Irishtown Bend.
- **S** Steve Olin and Tim Crews.

AE What type of stone was used to build the original section of the Cleveland Museum of Art in 1916?

B Electrical and telephone cables make up what Mayfield company's product line?

G This covered reservoir located on the East Side is supported by 1,196 columns spaced 18 feet apart and is believed to be the largest of its kind in the world. Name it.

H Why was Safety Director Eliot Ness forced to resign from his position in March of 1942?

S What event did the city hope to attract by building Cleveland Municipal Stadium?

AE White Georgian Marble.

B Preformed Line Products Co.

G The Baldwin Reservoir, which feeds the Baldwin Filtration Plant and Fairmount Pumping Station.

H For his involvement in a hit-and-run accident on the West Shoreway.

S The 1932 Olympics.

AE Name the Case Western Reserve University professor who dispenses parenting advice on her National Public Radio call-in show.

B What was the first product sold by Solon's Murphy-Phoenix Co., now a division of the Colgate Palmolive Co.?

G Which suburb lost 294 acres to a U. S. government bomber plant in 1942?

H The city of Cleveland annexed what in 1854?

S What Browns defensive player holds the team record for most career interceptions?

A

AE   Dr. Sylvia Rimm.

B   Murphy's Oil soap.

G   Middleburg Heights.

H   Ohio City.

S   Thom Darden, with 45.

AE What popular afternoon TV show hosted by Don Webster and originally called "The Big 5 Show" featured the last performance by Otis Redding?

B Before it switched to polymer production in the 1980s, what had been the primary business of the M. A. Hanna Co. since the 1840s?

G The Sheraton Cleveland City Centre hotel at E. 6th St. and St. Clair Ave. was formerly known by what name?

H According to accounts in the local papers, what great American philosopher and scholar received only lukewarm reviews for his lectures here in 1859?

S What native Clevelander owns the most successful team in Indy-Car-Racing history?

AE "Upbeat" on WEWS TV5.

B The mining of iron ore.

G The Bond Court Hotel.

H Ralph Waldo Emerson.

S Roger Penske.

AE What Oscar-winning special-effects wizard appeared in person to present his film clips and original models at the Cleveland Cinematheque in May 1993?

B Current New York Yankees owner George Steinbrenner became CEO of what Cleveland company in 1967?

G Cleveland's position as Ohio's most important shipping center was assured when which two bodies of water were connected by canal in the 1830s?

H What three long-standing Cleveland retail institutions whose names all started with "H" have met their demise since 1981?

S What was the Richfield Coliseum's inaugural event?

AE Ray Harryhausen.

B American Ship Building Co., an ore boat builder.

G Lake Erie and the Ohio River.

H Halle's, Higbee's, and Hough Bakery.

S A Frank Sinatra concert.

AE Name the young movie star who required police protection from a mob of 500+ teenagers while in town to promote his new film *White Feather* in 1955.

B What two labor groups were led by Patrick O'Malley from the 1950s through 1970?

G St. Clair Ave., one of Cleveland's oldest streets, is named for a former Northwest Territory governor. Name him.

H What event drew thousands of spectators from Ohio and Pennsylvania to Public Square on the night of April 29, 1879?

S Which Indians pitcher holds the team record of 266 career victories?

AE   Robert Wagner.

B   United Auto Workers and the Cleveland AFL-CIO.

G   Arthur St. Clair (1734-1818).

H   A demonstration of the first street lighting in the U.S., Charles F. Brush's arc lights.

S   Bob Feller (1936-56).

Q

AE What 1989 film by former Clevelander David Ward featured a hapless Cleveland Indians team that became surprise champions?

B Which was the last of Cleveland's three VHF TV stations to go on the air, in 1949?

G Name the lakefront development of highrise apartment buildings that includes Winton Place, The Carlyle, and The Waterford.

H What Alaskan hero spent his last six years in Cleveland before dying on March 14, 1933?

S What was the outcome of the first hockey game played at Richfield Coliseum by the Crusaders?

A

AE *Major League.*

B WJW TV8.

G The Gold Coast.

H Balto the sled dog.

S The game was postponed due to melting ice.

Q

AE What future late-night TV host took calls from panicked WGAR-AM listeners after the station's 1938 broadcast of "War of the Worlds"?

B This Cleveland-based company startled competitors in 1880 when it first marketed ready-mixed paint. Name it.

G The area bounded east to west by E. 79th to E. 27th, and north to south by Payne and Carnegie is known by what name?

H After studying the conditions of the site planned for Cleveland, what founding father claimed it was "the place at which an important city was to arise"?

S Who was the first black player in the American League, signed by the Cleveland Indians in 1947?

A

AE Jack Paar (later of "The Tonight Show" fame).

B Sherwin-Williams Co.

G The Midtown Corridor.

H Benjamin Franklin.

S Larry Doby.

AE   What Cleveland-born science fiction writer, a major contributor to the original "Star Trek" and "The Twilight Zone" series has won more awards in the field of imaginative literature than any other writer?

B   One of the first built in a Cleveland suburb, this residential hotel was placed on the National Register of Historic Places in 1979. Name it.

G   Name Tremont's four streets with "educational" names (from its days as home to Cleveland University, the city's first, but short-lived (1851-53), institution of higher learning).

H   During the late 1850s, when he was between the ages of 10 and 14, what legendary Wild West figure resided on his family's property near Euclid Ave. and E. 83rd St.?

S   What NBA standout played third base for Toronto when Indians pitcher Len Barker pitched a 1981 perfect game against Toronto?

AE Harlan Ellison.

B The Alcazar Hotel in Cleveland Heights.

G University Rd., Professor St., College Ave., and Literary Ave.

H William F. "Buffalo Bill" Cody.

S Danny Ainge.

AE What silent movie premiered at the Allen Theater on April 1, 1921, accompanied by a $40,000 pipe organ?

B Who makes Nut-Mallos candy?

G Hessler Court is the last remaining street in Cleveland paved with what material?

H In 1899, Coburn Haskell, member of The Country Club, Joseph Mitchell, pro at The Country Club, and Bertram Work, of the B.F. Goodrich Corp., developed what innovation that changed the game of golf?

S What is the nickname of David N. Myers College (formerly Dyke College) sports teams?

A

AE *The Greatest Love.*

B Malley's Chocolates.

G Wood.

H The wound-rubber-core golf ball.

S The Demons.

AE The nation's oldest continuing regional theater company was founded in 1916. What is its name?

B What cartoon character, first syndicated in 1969, was dreamed up by a young artist working as an intern at American Greetings?

G What street was known as "Millionaire's Row" at the turn of the century?

H What industrialist and financier, for whom a local theater was later named, played the leading role in a local 1873 production of *Mr. Pickwick and his Friends*, based on the novel by Charles Dickens?

S Who coached the CSU Viking basketball team to a 1986 berth in the NCAA tournament?

AE The Cleveland Play House.

B "Ziggy," by Lakewood resident Tom Wilson.

G Euclid Ave.

H Marcus A. Hanna.

S Kevin Mackey.

AE What Michael Stanley song was covered by Joe Walsh on his 1985 album, *The Confessor*?

B Name the historic architectural firm, active from 1897 to 1939, that designed such Cleveland landmarks as the Cleveland Museum of Art, the West Side Market, the YMCA Building, and Wade Chapel in Lake View Cemetery.

G Excavation for which interstate uncovered Dunkleosteus, a genus of large armored fish found in the Cleveland Shale?

H Which church is Cleveland's oldest religious structure and once served as a hideout on the underground railroad?

S In 1991, the Indians pulled off one of the most lopsided trades in recent history when they traded catcher Ed Taubensee and pitcher Willie Blair to the Houston Astros for third baseman Dave Rohde and what future All-Star outfielder?

A

AE "Rosewood Bitters."

B Hubbell & Benes.

G I-71 (in the summer of 1965).

H St. John's Episcopal Church.

S Kenny Lofton.

AE RKO Palace Theater brought in the Marx Brothers' show to compete for audiences with neighboring Hanna Theater's 1930 production, "Sex," starring what buxom and bawdy Hollywood star?

B What Cleveland company created "The Playboy," an upscale touring car that was advertised in women's magazines?

G Within 10, what is the number of cloudy days in a typical Cleveland year?

H The City Planning Commission gave what title to the two massive master planning documents prepared for the city's downtown core and neighborhoods during Mayor George Voinovich's administration?

S Prior to the 1994 season, Indians General Manager John Hart cemented the Tribe infield by trading what two players for Seattle shortstop Omar Vizquel?

AE Mae West.

B The Jordan Motor Car Co.

G 201.8 (based on statistics recorded over a 53-year period.)

H Civic Vision 2000.

S Shortstop Felix Fermin and first baseman Reggie Jefferson.

AE What seminal British heavy metal group kicked off its first U.S. tour in almost two years at sold-out Richfield Coliseum in 1975?

B Until it merged into Society Corp. in 1986, by what name was Centran Corp. better known?

G Name the three remaining downtown arcades.

H What Clevelander was instrumental in founding the Western Union Telegraph Co. and later served as its president?

S What 1970s Browns All-Star defensive lineman nearly died from a staph infection?

AE Led Zeppelin.

B Central National Bank.

G The Old Arcade, the Colonial Arcade, and the Euclid Arcade.

H Jeptha Homer Wade I.

S Jerry Sherk.

AE The Cleveland Orchestra's home at Severance Hall was built in 1931 as a memorial to whom?

B Lezius-Hiles Co. was a: A) men's haberdashery; B) bed manufacturer; C) tool and die company; D) printing firm.

G This tourist rail service operates on old Baltimore & Ohio Railroad track between Independence and Akron. Name it.

H What opened in 1870, creating employment for many Italian stoneworkers who immigrated to the area now known as Little Italy?

S Whom did the Indians trade to the Boston Red Sox in 1978 in return for pitcher Rick Wise, pitcher Mike Paxton, catcher Bo Diaz, and outfielder/infielder Ted Cox?

AE Elizabeth DeWitt Severance, wife of philanthropist John L. Severance.

B D) printing firm.

G The Cuyahoga Valley Scenic Railroad (formerly the Cuyahoga Valley Line).

H Lake View Cemetery.

S Pitcher Dennis Eckersley.

AE The fourth-oldest museum of Judaica in the U.S., containing a 40,000-volume library and collections of religious art and artifacts, is located in University Circle. What is its name?

B In 1960, *The Plain Dealer* moved into the home of what former Forest City Publishing Co. sibling paper?

G What building is home to the renowned Cleveland Orchestra?

H On July 22, 1946, 200,000 spectators turned out to see the Army Air Force show, fireworks, and illuminated regatta that were part of what event?

S Where did Cavs great Bingo Smith attend college?

AE Temple Museum of Religious Art.

B *The Cleveland News.*

G Severance Hall.

H The Cleveland Sesquicentennial Celebration.

S The University of Tulsa.

AE The building housing the Cleveland Center for Contemporary Art, located at 8501 Carnegie, was originally a warehouse for what national department store chain?

B What's the signature product of Royal Appliance Manufacturing Co.?

G Western Reserve College moved from what village to Cleveland in 1882?

H In which Cleveland disaster did inventor Garrett A. Morgan demonstrate the effectiveness of his recently patented gas mask by strapping it on and using it while rescuing victims?

S What two former Browns players went on to coach multiple Super-Bowl-winning teams?

AE   Sears and Roebuck.

B   The Dirt Devil vacuum.

G   Hudson.

H   The Cleveland Waterworks explosion of July 25, 1916.

S   Don Shula with the Miami Dolphins, and Chuck Noll with the Pittsburgh Steelers.

AE What alternative rock star, who won a Grammy Award in 1992 for best heavy metal performance, supported his music career in Cleveland in the early 1980s by scrubbing toilets?

B To pull the city out of default by reducing administrative costs, this mayor organized a task force of executives from private industry; it became the forerunner of Cleveland's Public-Private Partnerships program. Name him.

G What are the latitude and longitude of downtown Cleveland?

H In 1892, after assuming the pulpit of the Tifereth Israel Congregation (later The Temple), Rabbi Moses J. Gries was responsible for creating what radical new approach to the Jewish faith?

S During the "Miracle of Richfield" playoff run in 1976, what team did the Cavaliers beat with three baskets in the last seconds of the game?

AE Trent Reznor of Nine Inch Nails.

B George Voinovich.

G Latitude N. 41° 29′ 51″; Longitude W. 81° 41′ 50″

H The world's first "open temple," in which anyone interested in religious, educational, and cultural activities was welcome.

S The Washington Bullets.

AE Daytime talk show host Phil Donahue attended what area high school?

B At what Lorain Rd. restaurant did Cleveland Mayor Dennis Kucinich eat his daily breakfast of steak and eggs?

G Name the three main parks comprising Cleveland Lakefront State Park.

H What controversial West Coast law enforcement official was brought in as Chief of Police only to be abruptly fired by Mayor Kucinich shortly after moving to Cleveland?

S On August 16, 1920, what Indians player was struck dead by a pitch, becoming the first and only major league player to die while on the field?

AE St. Edward High School in Lakewood.

B Mr. Z's.

G Edgewater Park, Gordon Park, and Euclid Beach Park.

H Richard Hongisto.

S Shortstop Ray Chapman, who was beaned by Carl Mays of the Yankees at the New York Polo Grounds.

AE Which musical director of the Cleveland Orchestra was once director of the Hamburg State Opera?

B · Newman-Stern Co. was: A) a grocery store; B) a jewelry store; C) a sporting goods store?

G In what city are the Cuyahoga County Fairgrounds located?

H This Clevelander was the first woman elected to the Cuyahoga County Common Pleas court (1920) and the Ohio Supreme Court (1922). She became the first female chief judge of a U.S. federal court when sworn in as Chief Judge of the Sixth Circuit in 1958. Name her.

S What was the Cavs' record during their initial season?

AE Christoph von Dohnanyi.

B C) A sporting goods store.

G Berea.

H Florence E. Allen (1884-1966).

S 16 wins and 67 losses.

AE What Cleveland rap group went platinum with their 1994 debut recording, "Creepin' On Ah Come Up"?

B Complete this famous slogan created by Wyse Advertising: "With a name like Smuckers…"

G What was the district located near Broadway Ave. and E. 9th St. called?

H What Cleveland politician served as Secretary of Health, Education and Welfare for both the Kennedy and Johnson administrations?

S What two future stars were added to the Cavaliers in the same off-season as 1986 draft pick Brad Daugherty?

AE Bone Thugs 'N Harmony.

B …it has to be good."

G Haymarket district.

H Anthony J. Celebrezze.

S Ron Harper (eighth pick in draft) and Mark Price (from a trade with the Dallas Mavericks).

AE Since 1976, an annual event in Twinsburg has attracted the world's largest gathering of what?

B What weekly news publication chronicles the city's financial wheeling and dealing?

G Which downtown street spans only one block, from E. 6th St. to E. 9th St.?

H Founded in 1912, this club is one of the oldest ongoing forums for free speech in the nation. Name it.

S What famous baseball badboy and onetime Indians outfielder was fined $25 in 1960 for traveling 70 miles per hour on the Memorial Shoreway near Gordon Park?

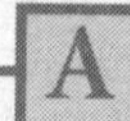

AE   Twins. (Twinsburg was founded by twin brothers Aaron and Moses Wilcox in 1827.)

B   *Crain's Cleveland Business*.

G   Vincent Ave. (popularly known as "Short Vincent" during its more notorious days of after-hours nightlife, gambling, and girlie bars).

H   The Cleveland City Club.

S   Billy Martin.

AE Formerly a full-time Cleveland Sanitation Dept. employee, this non-professional actor/comedian was the first African-American to join the regular staff at the Cleveland Play House. Name him.

B What major railroad freight line serves northeast Ohio?

G What U.S. government organization is located at 21000 Brookpark Rd.?

H With capacity for 1,000 passengers, what is the largest cruise ship on the Great Lakes?

S What Cavs player won the NBA All-Star Game Long Distance Shootout title in 1994?

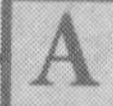

AE Nolan D. Bell (1920-1976). Bell is the only garbage collector ever to be listed in *Who's Who in America*.

B Conrail.

G NASA Lewis Research Center.

H *The Goodtime III*.

S Mark Price.

AE Name the father of "America's foremost musical family," who came to the U.S. from Czechoslovakia in 1884 and raised eight children, six of whom became members of the Cleveland Orchestra.

B This restaurant in Little Italy, founded in 1918, claims the distinction of being the oldest continuously operating Italian restaurant in Cleveland. Name it.

G The early (1900) subdivision on the western edge of present-day Cleveland Heights was once known by what name, after its original owner?

H Name the four military conflicts in which the Cleveland Grays fought.

S Name the first-ever opponent of the Cleveland Browns.

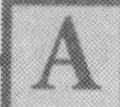

AE Frank Hruby (1856-1912).

B Guarino's, established by Italian immigrant Vincenzo Guarino.

G Ambler Heights, named for Dr. Nathan Hardy Ambler (1824-1888).

H Civil War, Spanish-American War, Mexican Border Dispute of 1916-17, World War I.

S The Miami Seahawks, who played the Browns on September 6, 1946.

AE What is the name of Cleveland's oldest existing literary discussion group, which has met twice a month for nine months out of the year since its founding in 1946?

B What company was created by the 1968 merger of Cleveland Twist Drill and National Acme Co.?

G Completed in 1939 and among the first in the nation, this public housing project is located at W. 28th st. near the Main Avenue Bridge. Name it.

H Karen Horn was the first female president of what institution?

S To whom did the Cleveland White Horses lose the first pro basketball game played in the Arena 32-29 in 1939?

AE Cleveland Heights's Great Books Group.

B Acme-Cleveland Corp.

G Lakeview Terrace.

H The Federal Reserve Bank of Cleveland. Horn was appointed in 1984. She was also the first female director of TRW, Inc.

S The Akron Firestones.

AE What Hollywood comedian and sitcom actor played the trumpet in the Rhodes High School band.

B Bob Feller pitches for what Cleveland investment firm?

G What architect designed Mather Mansion, Trinity Cathedral, the Union Club, and the four stone bridges in Rockefeller Park?

H What are the first names of the two Van Sweringen brothers, who built the Terminal Tower complex in the 1920s?

S While attending Syracuse University, Jim Brown became the first collegiate double All American. In what two sports was he honored?

AE Drew Carey.

B McDonald & Co. Securities Inc.

G Charles F. Schweinfurth (1856-1919).

H Oris and Mantis.

S Football and lacrosse.

AE Public TV station WVIZ airs an annual fundraising auction. What is that auction's mascot?

B What brewery, regarded as Cleveland's oldest when it closed permanently in 1958, produced Black Dallas malt liquor, "World Series Special" beer, and had delivery trucks whose horns sounded the tune "How Dry I Am"?

G In what Cleveland neighborhood did George Voinovich live while mayor?

H Which hospital was the first established in a Cleveland suburb? (It still operates on the original site.)

S Indians pitcher Steve Dunning beat the Oakland A's in May of 1971 by becoming the most recent pitcher in the AL to accomplish what feat?

AE A zebra.

B The Leisy Brewing Co. (originally named Isaac Leisy & Co.), established ca. 1873.

G Collinwood.

H Lakewood Hospital, which opened in 1907 with three doctors and fifteen beds in a double frame house on Detroit and Belle avenues.

S He hit a grand slam.

AE Name the Brahmsian-bearded violinist who played for the Cleveland Orchestra from 1957 until his death in 1995, just a few weeks before his scheduled retirement?

B Active Communications, Inc., founded in 1988 by brothers Ken and Ron McEntee, publishes what humor-oriented monthly?

G In 1930 the Cleveland Metroparks opened the nation's first trailside museum in which reservation?

H Moses Cleaveland was not the only city founder to lose an "a" from his name. The name of what other local founding father is borne by three Cleveland suburbs, but without the extra "a"?

S Who was covering Chicago Bull Michael Jordan during the 1989 playoffs when he hit "the Shot" to win the series?

AE Leonard Samuels.

B *The Weekly Farce* (published monthly despite its title and completely written by the McEntees).

G North Chagrin Reservation.

H Aaron Olmstead.

S Craig Ehlo.

AE Which of these musical talents did not perform at the Rock and Roll Hall of Fame and Museum opening concert on September 2, 1995? A) Bruce Springsteen; B) Johnny Cash; C) Bon Jovi; D) Jerry Lee Lewis; E) Hootie and the Blowfish; F) Al Green; G) Aretha Franklin; H) The Kinks; I) Little Richard J) Chuck Berry.

B For a brief time during the Great Depression, what bygone Cleveland truck maker merged with Studebaker?

G Murray Hill at Mayfield Rd. is known as Little Italy. Where was Big Italy?

H What disaster in May of 1929 led to the development of safer standards for storage and labeling of x-ray film?

S Who was the first coach of the Cavaliers?

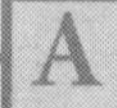

AE E) Hootie and the Blowfish.

B White Motor Corp.

G Lower Central-Woodland district.

H The Cleveland Clinic fire, in which 123 people lost their lives.

S Bill Fitch.

AE This musical playwright was born in Berea and performed at age nine in the Berea Summer Theater at Baldwin-Wallace. He later composed the award-winning musical *Godspell* while a graduate student. Name him.

B "Big Ginger" was a spokesmodel for what Cleveland bottling company?

G The residents of Slavic Village north of Broadway are predominantly of Czech and Slavic descent. Residents south of Broadway belong mostly to what ethnic group?

H She became the first woman in the world to head a major urban public library when she was appointed as the fourth head librarian of the Cleveland Public Library. Name her.

S Who holds the American League record for most strikeouts by a rookie pitcher?

AE John-Michael Tebelak.

B Cotton Club Bottling & Canning Co.

G Polish.

H Linda Anne Eastman (1867-1963).

S Herb Score, who struck out 245 batters in 1955.

AE What theater, once known as "Handsomest playhouse on Detroit Ave.," is being restored by Cleveland Public Theatre?

B What now-defunct construction company built the Terminal Tower?

G Where can you find the eight "Guardians of Traffic"?

H After being found not guilty of murdering his wife Marilyn in a second trial in 1966, Dr. Sam Sheppard was readmitted to the practice of osteopathic medicine, but later left to pursue what part-time career?

S Name any Browns player signed from the USFL following its demise in 1986.

AE Gordon Square Theatre.

B John Gill & Sons.

G On the Hope Memorial (Lorain-Carnegie) Bridge. (They are the giant human figures carved in the bridge's sandstone pylons.)

H Professional wrestling.

S Mike Johnson, Dan Fike, Frank Minnifield, Kevin Mack, and Gerald McNeil.

AE What was the last name of Gene Carroll's partner on the popular radio show "Gene and Glenn"?

B The old Cleveland Rolling Mill plant is now known by what name?

G Where is the only public polo field in Cuyahoga County?

H Who was the only newspaper reporter to arrive for work at *The Cleveland Press* in a chauffeur-driven Rolls Royce?

S In 1960, Indian General Manager Frank Lane traded Joe Gordon for Detroit's Jimmie Dykes. What was unusual about this trade?

AE   Glenn Rowell.

B   American Steel & Wire Co.

G   In the Cleveland Metroparks South Chagrin Reservation.

H   Winsor French.

S   Gordon and Dykes were managers.

Q

AE Name the Cleveland-born writer who used a portable Royal on trains and in hotel rooms to create the adventures of his comic book hero.

B In 1929, aviation pioneer Glenn L. Martin moved his airplane manufacturing company from Cleveland to Baltimore. What is the name of the company today?

G The record for the heaviest local snowfall was broken in 1995–96. What winter season held the previous record?

H In honor of the colony by which it had initially been claimed, the Western Reserve was also known by what name?

S In addition to the Cleveland Cavaliers, what other professional sports team did Ted Stepien own?

AE Jerry Siegel, creator of Superman.

B Lockheed-Marietta Corp.

G 1981-82 (100.5 inches).

H New Connecticut.

S The Cleveland Competitors, a professional softball team that played in the United Pro Softball League. It folded in 1982.

AE What film clocked in at 25 hours and 32 minutes to become the longest film ever shown at the Cleveland Cinematheque?

B What Cleveland-based company, established in 1881, gained fame as a manufacturer of telescopes and optical instruments, although most of its financial success came through the production of machine tools such as turret lathes?

G E. 55th St., considered the "unofficial" division point between downtown and the East Side, was formerly known by what name?

H What were the names of the first two main streets laid out in Moses Cleaveland's original surveying party plan for the city?

S Upon purchasing the Cavs in 1980, whom did Ted Stepien hire to be the head coach?

AE Reitz's *Heimat II (Die Zweite Heimat)*.

B Warner and Swasey Co.

G Willson St.

H Superior and Ontario.

S Bill Musselman.

AE What is the name of the Cleveland Orchestra's summer home, and what family is it named after?

B What nonprofit organization promotes the revitalization of Cleveland's near East Side?

G Where does Case Western Reserve Medical School bury the remains of persons who have donated their bodies to science?

H For fear it would be destroyed in wartime coastal raids on the capital, the National Medical Library was temporarily relocated to what Cleveland facility in 1942?

S In 1901, what team beat the Cleveland Blues 8-2 to win the first American League baseball game?

AE The Blossom Music Center was named in honor of the Dudley S. Blossom family, who donated $1.3 million toward its construction.

B Midtown Corridor, Inc.

G Riverside Cemetery, on Pearl Rd.

H The Howard Dittrick Museum of Medical History, in the Allen Memorial Library on the CWRU campus.

S The Chicago Whitestockings.

AE The fourth and final World Series of Rock on August 23, 1975 at Cleveland Municipal Stadium was attended by 65,000 fans. Who were the event's four headliners?

B Which Cleveland UHF station, established in 1968, was directly affiliated with a Hollywood movie production company?

G In the 1920s, the area centered at E. 55th St. and Woodland Ave. was home to large numbers of which ethnic group? A) Russians; B) Poles; C) African-Americans; D) Italians.

H Born in Concord Township in 1858, what gentleman claimed to have discovered Columbus' landing spot in the Bahamas, made four tries at reaching the North Pole, and attempted to cross the Atlantic in a dirigible?

S What two local colleges play in the Ohio Athletic Conference?

AE Rod Stewart, Uriah Heep, Blue Oyster Cult, and Aerosmith.

B WUAB TV43. Its parent company was United Artists.

G A) Russians.

H Walter Wellman.

S The Baldwin-Wallace Yellow Jackets and the John Carroll Blue Streaks.

AE Name the blue-eyed movie star (and spaghetti-sauce maker) who was raised in Shaker Heights.

B What dry goods store used to occupy the site of Great Lakes Brewing Co.?

G What stunning Russian Orthodox Cathedral, now on the National Register of Historic Places, is located on Starkweather Ave. in Tremont?

H Although Cleveland was a Republican stronghold at the time, what famous politician was given a hostile reception on September 3, 1866, by the Republican Party here because they opposed his approach to Reconstruction?

5 What are Big Met and Little Met?

AE Paul Newman.

B Fries & Schuele Co.

G St. Theodosius.

H President Andrew Johnson.

S Golf Courses in the Metroparks Rocky River Reservation.

AE What author, born in Cleveland in 1858 to former slaves, was the first black writer to examine issues of race and equality in his novels and short stories?

B Nathan Dauby was a successful shoe merchant when he went to work for this company in 1904; he later built it into the largest department store in Ohio. Name it.

G From the Inner Belt, which exit would you take to get to Tremont?

H In what year did the Cuyahoga River most recently catch fire?

S What was the name of Cleveland's professional basketball team in 1944?

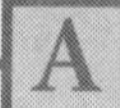

AE   Charles Waddell Chesnutt (1858-1932). Chesnutt was also a lawyer and court stenographer.

B   The May Company (now known as Kaufmann's).

G   W. 14th St. / Abbey Ave. exit.

H   1969. It had previously burned in 1952.

S   The Cleveland Chase Brass Basketball Squad.

AE By what mode of transportation did Charles Dickens arrive in Cleveland in 1842?

B H.W. Beattie and Sons is what type of retailer? A) shoes; B) jewelry; C) ladies' hats.

G What was the former name of the Cleveland Botanical Garden?

H The Five Mile Crib is five miles from what?

S Name the Browns players associated with the following retired numbers: 14, 32, 45, 46, 76.

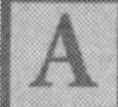

AE Steamship. (The *Constitution* brought Dickens here from Sandusky.)

B B) jewelry

G The Garden Center of Greater Cleveland.

H The Kirtland pumping station, near Bratenahl.

S Otto Graham, Jim Brown, Ernie Davis, Don Fleming, Lou Groza.

AE Who was the longtime host of "Polka Varieties"?

B What Euclid manufacturer of welding equipment is nationally known for its unusual employee incentive/bonus system?

G Which Cleveland nightclub was the original site of the popular free "coffee break concerts"?

H Established in 1914, this philanthropic organization was the pioneer community trust in the United States. Name it.

S What other sporting event was held in Cleveland on the same day in 1981 that welterweight champion Roberto Duran beat Mike Nino Gonzalez in a fight held at Public Hall?

AE Paul Wilcox.

B Lincoln Electric Co.

G Cleveland Agora.

H The Cleveland Foundation.

S The Baseball All-Star Game.

AE Name the *Plain Dealer* Radio and TV Editor who wrote the book *Cleveland: The Best Kept Secret*.

B In 1964, Pittway Corp., a real estate and manufacturing concern, bought what Cleveland publishing business?

G Where can you find Ohio's largest natural sandy beach and the last remaining natural sand dunes along the shore of Lake Erie?

H True or false: Carl Stokes was the first African-American mayor in the state of Ohio.

S By what mode of transportation did the inaugural foursome for Lake Forest Country Club in Hudson reach the first tee?

AE George E. Condon.

B Penton Publishing.

G Headlands Beach State Park in Mentor.

H False. That honor belongs to Robert Henry, elected mayor of Springfield in 1965.

S Goodyear Blimp. (The foursome included Walter Hagen, Tommy Armour, Horton Smith, and Densmore Shute.)

AE Cleveland native Ernest Tidyman wrote the screenplay (and the novel on which it was based) for what trend-setting early 1970s action film?

B An early 1980s civic marketing campaign compared Cleveland to what fruit?

G John M. Coyne holds the record for longest continuous term of service by any mayor in the nation. Of what West Side municipality is he the mayor?

H Noted Cleveland researcher Dr. James H. Salisbury (1823-1905) pioneered the research of germs and the relation of food and drink to disease. What dish did he create and prescribe in his cures?

S What two former Indians players have last names that are palindromes (spelled the same way forward and backward)?

AE *Shaft.*

B A plum.

G Brooklyn. (Coyne has served since 1946.)

H Salisbury Steak.

S Toby Harrah and Dave Otto.

AE Name the Cleveland-born actress who received Oscar nominations for her roles in *Terms of Endearment* and *An Officer and a Gentleman.*

B The "Webster" duster is made by what northeast Ohio company?

G What law-enforcement division is headquartered at E. 38th St. and S. Marginal Rd.?

H Name the architectural firm that designed all these Cleveland landmarks: Public Auditorium, the Federal Reserve Bank, the Cleveland Public Library, Municipal Stadium, and Severance Hall.

S What Browns wide receiver, drafted in 1986 out of Colorado, was also drafted by the NBA and MLB?

A

AE Debra Winger.

B Sunshine Industries.

G Cleveland Mounted Police.

H Walker & Weeks.

S Dave Logan.

AE This national music monthly based in Cleveland celebrated its 10th anniversary in 1995.

B Which downtown retail complex, renovated and rebuilt from the former Union Station facility, opened in 1990?

G What is the fourth tallest building in Cleveland?

H William A. Stinchcomb instituted what county wide district in 1915?

S Whom did Art Modell name as head football coach after firing Paul Brown in 1963?

AE *Alternative Press.*

B The Avenue at Tower City.

G Erieview Tower.

H The Cleveland Metropolitan Parks District, now known as Cleveland Metroparks. (Stinchcomb was Cleveland Parks director.)

S Blanton Collier.

AE What rock group was banned from Cleveland for 18 months by mayor Ralph J. Perk after fans stormed the Public Hall stage, halting their performance for 10 minutes?

B What name does this Cleveland suit maker, born in 1845 as Koch & Loeb, now wear?

G Which Cleveland neighborhood hosts the Greek Heritage Festival?

H Who proposed housing delegates in ships on Lake Erie in an attempt to attract a political convention to the city?

S From whom did Nick Mileti purchase the Indians in 1972?

A

AE The Beatles.

B Joseph & Feiss.

G Tremont.

H Mayor Ralph J. Perk.

S Vernon Stouffer.

AE Cleveland's African-American Museum was one of the first such museums to open in the country—in what year?

B What local company is a major producer of frit, an ingredient in porcelain enamel and ceramic glazes?

G Founded as a "company town" in the 1890s by the Austin Powder Co., this southeast Cuyahoga County village was the last county municipality to levy an income tax on its residents. Name it.

H Where was Cleveland gangster Danny Greene coming from when he was permanently "excised" by a car bomb parked next to his vehicle?

S What Browns quarterback set an NFL record for completion percentage, going 21-23 in a game against the Rams?

A

AE 1953.

B Ferro Corp.

G Glenwillow.

H His dentist.

S Vinny Testaverde, in December 1993.

AE What nonprofit group founded in 1978 promotes "the musical art form born in America"?

B Peanut-butter-and-onion burgers are a house specialty at what West Side restaurant?

G What name describes the area on Fleet Ave. between E. 55th and E. 65th streets, once dubbed "Warszawa"?

H In 1951, APCOA opened what type of facility at Cleveland Hopkins Airport that was the first of its kind in the U.S.?

S In 1977, what Cleveland Indian pitched 22 1/3 consecutive hitless innings, only 2/3 innings short of the record set by Cy Young?

AE The Northeast Ohio Jazz Society.

B Bearden's in Rocky River.

G Slavic Village.

H Paid parking lots.

S Dennis Eckersley.

AE What legendary early rock 'n' roller was an avowed Cleveland Browns fan?

B What Cleveland company made flavoring extracts before it began blending and bottling distilled liquors?

G Which is the largest gem in the "Emerald Neck-lace"?

H The Port of Cleveland is closer to Europe than many ports along the mid-Atlantic coast. True or false?

S Who was the Cleveland women's track star who once held world records in the 220- and 100-yard dashes in the mid-1930s?

AE Elvis Presley.

B Paramount Distillers Inc.

G Rocky River Reservation is the largest of the Cleveland Metroparks.

H True.

S Stella Walsh.

AE Bruce Springsteen wrote the title song to what movie set in Cleveland and starring Joan Jett and Michael J. Fox as a brother and sister in a rock band?

B According to the ad jingle, where can you see Commander Ray?

G What street fair takes place on Euclid Ave. the first weekend in June?

H In 1949, a plane competing in the National Air Races crashed into a residential home in what suburb?

S What was the name given by onetime Browns owner Mickey McBride to the second- and third-string players who drove cabs for his Zone Cab company during their off hours?

AE *Light of Day.*

B "At West Park Chevrolet."

G Square to Square (From Public Square to Playhouse Square).

H Berea. (The pilot and two residents were killed).

S "Taxi Squad."

AE What actor charmed children with his television show "Barnaby" for more than 20 years?

B Prior to Prohibition, what company's "Cleveland" beer was promoted with the slogan "A Wonderful City—A Wonderful Beer."?

G On what street is Cleveland's Greyhound Bus Station located?

H Artemus Ward, whom many consider "the father of American humor," was the pen name used by what writer who lived and worked here from 1857 to 1860?

S In 1980, what Brush High graduate won the Cy Young Award as a pitcher for the Baltimore Orioles?

AE Linn Sheldon.

B Gund Brewing Co.

G Chester Ave.

H Charles Farrar Browne.

S Steve Stone.

AE What children's vocal group with a heavenly name has represented Cleveland at the White House, the Vatican, and the Great Wall of China?

B What Cleveland company introduced the round ice cream carton?

G Name the site where Moses Cleaveland's surveying party is believed to have first touched ground?

H What religious visionary experienced a revelation instructing his followers in western New York to "assemble together in Ohio," at Kirtland?

S Who was the Tribe's youngest player of all time?

AE The Singing Angels.

B Pierre's French Ice Cream Co.

G Settler's Landing in the Flats.

H Mormon leader Joseph Smith.

S Bob Feller, at the age of 17 in 1936.

AE What Cathedral Latin High School graduate and former *Plain Dealer* reporter became Hollywood's highest-paid screen writer in the 1980s?

B In 1958, what Cleveland company merged with Ramo-Woolridge Corp. of California to form TRW?

G What three locations were home to the Great American Rib Cook-Off before it moved to Burke Lakefront Airport?

H What book about Cleveland and Cuyahoga County, first published in 1987, was the first of its kind in the field of urban history?

S Name the Cleveland Lumberjacks' mascot.

AE Joe Eszterhas.

B Thompson Products Co.

G Berea Fairgrounds, Mall C on Public Square, and North Coast Harbor.

H *The Encyclopedia of Cleveland History*, edited by CWRU history professors David D. Van Tassel and John J. Grabowski.

S Buzz the beaver.

AE In what year did the Cleveland Orchestra complete its first European tour, triumphantly returning to a crowd of cheering fans?

B This company's trombones, trumpets, and clarinets have been blown by the likes of Tommy Dorsey and the rock group Chicago. Name it.

G Formerly the village of S. Newburgh, this suburb adopted its current name from a park located within its boundaries. Name it.

H Fenn College is now part of what educational institution?

S What Browns quarterback holds the NFL record for most consecutive passes thrown without an interception?

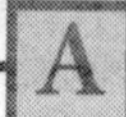

AE 1957.

B King Musical Instruments.

G Garfield Heights takes its name from Garfield Park, formerly Newburgh Park, which was renamed for James A. Garfield in 1897.

H Cleveland State University.

S Bernie Kosar, who threw 308 passes without an interception in 1990-91.

AE In what language does Lyric Opera Cleveland perform?

B Founded as the Sandusky Portland Cement Co. in 1892, what Cleveland Heights company derives its current name from Greek mythology?

G In the mid-1800s, what downtown intersection was so muddy and rutted from stagecoach wheels that it was called "the frog pond"?

H Which presidential candidate stopped at Hellriegel's restaurant in Painesville while campaigning for the 1960 election?

S What former Cleveland broadcaster is regarded nationally as the "Father of Sports Talk Radio"?

AE   English.

B   Medusa Corp.

G   Euclid Ave. and Erie (E. 9th) St.

H   John F. Kennedy.

S   Pete Franklin.

AE On what afternoon TV movie show could Clevelanders phone in to win a modest jackpot from host John Lanigan?

B This manufacturing facility on Coit Rd. was the site of the initial sit-down strike (in Dec. 1936) against General Motors which eventually led to the recognition of the United Auto Workers in Feb. 1937. Name it.

G Where is Cleveland's City Mission?

H In 1961, she became the first woman to run for mayor of Cleveland but lost to Anthony J. Celebrezze. Name her.

S What was the name of the first Cleveland indoor soccer team?

AE WUAB TV43's "Prize Movie."

B GM's Fisher Body Plant.

G E. 55th & Carnegie.

H Albina Cermak (1904-1978).

S The Cleveland Force (1978 to 1988).

AE What internationally acclaimed architect designed the Rock and Roll Hall of Fame and Museum building?

B What coffee company has been roasting at W. 29th & Detroit since 1930?

G "The Silver Chisel" is its nickname. What is its real name?

H What was the title of William Ganson Rose's definitive history of Cleveland, published in 1950?

S What league-wide rule did the NBA institute as a result of the poor management practices of onetime Cavalier owner Ted Stepien?

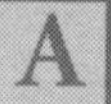

AE I.M. Pei.

B Van Rooy Coffee Co.

G One Cleveland Center.

H *Cleveland: The Making of a City*.

S An NBA franchise cannot trade two consecutive years' first round draft choices.

AE What radio station is known as "The Home of the Buzzard"?

B What are the first names of the founding partners of the law firm, Squire, Sanders and Dempsey?

G During his tenure as mayor, what was George Voinovich's first neighborhood revitalization program?

H What literary-social group, formed in 1838 by William Case and Leonard Case, Jr., met in a small office on Public Square adorned with stuffed animals and snakes?

S Who were the "Big Four" starting pitchers who led the 1954 Indians team to a major league baseball record of 111 wins?

AE WMMS-FM.

B Andrew, William, and James.

G The Lexington Village housing project.

H "The Arkites." Members shared an interest in natural sciences and culture.

S Bob Feller, Bob Lemon, Early Wynn, Mike Garcia.

AE Cleveland is the hometown of this pornography czar famed for showing up at court in Groucho glasses or other comic disguises. Who is he?

B What legendary downtown bookstore was run by Ann and Bob Levine until the late 1970s?

G What area was once considered the Greenhouse Capital of Cleveland?

H Name the 1836 conflict culminating in the heated competition between Ohio City (West Side) and Cleveland (East Side).

S Name the Clevelander who won the featherweight boxing title by defeating Abe Attell in a 20-round bout in 1912.

AE Reuben Sturman.

B Publix Book Mart.

G Old Brooklyn.

H The "Bridge War."

S Johnny Kilbane.

AE What fiery rock singer, associated with the "psychedelic era" in San Francisco, donated her fringed vest to the Rock and Roll Hall of Fame and Museum?

B What Cleveland family business got its start fixing Model-T tires in 1918?

G Between 1900 and 1914, this neighborhood had the largest concentration of Hungarians outside of Hungary. Name it.

H This civil rights leader was scheduled to appear in Cleveland to recruit marchers for the Poor People's campaign only six days after his assassination. Who was he?

S What former Browns head coach played on Vince Lombardi's championship Green Bay Packer teams?

A

AE Grace Slick.

B Mueller Tire.

G The Buckeye-Woodland community.

H Rev. Dr. Martin Luther King, Jr.

S Forrest Gregg.

AE Name at least three pop/rock songs that mention the word "Cleveland" in the title.

B Who are "The Sunshine People"?

G City Council passed an ordinance in 1861 giving Public Square what new name?

H In what year was Cuyahoga County created?

S In 1920, the Cleveland Tigers of the American Professional Football Association (forerunner to the NFL) ended the season with a losing record after what captain/star player suffered an injury?

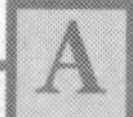

AE "Cleveland Now," Booker T. and the MG's; "There's No Surf in Cleveland," Euclid Beach Band; "Cleveland Rocks," Ian Hunter; "Let's Move to Cleveland," Frank Zappa; "Look Out Cleveland," The Band.

B The East Ohio Gas Co.

G Monumental Park (in recognition of a memorial to Commodore Perry, which was later moved).

H 1807.

S Jim Thorpe.

AE Where were the ballpark scenes for the movie *Major League* filmed?

B The first feasible artificial kidney was developed at what Cleveland hospital?

G Cleveland's rapid transit system was the first in the country to provide a direct rail connection between the downtown business district and what other facility?

H This organization, started as The Cleveland Community Fund, pioneered the practice of asking companies to encourage their employees to contribute a percentage of their income to charity. Name it.

S What Indians owner created Joe Early Day, Ladies' Night, and Fireworks Night?

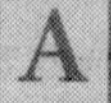

AE County Stadium in Milwaukee.

B The Cleveland Clinic.

G The airport.

H United Way.

S Bill Veeck, owner from 1946 to 1949.

AE In 1986, a parody song about Browns quarterback Bernie Kosar hit the top of Cleveland's music charts. On what famous oldies tune was "Bernie, Bernie" based?

B Name the family-owned grocery store chain that started as a Shaker Heights butcher shop in 1929.

G What city has Cuyahoga County's highest point of elevation?

H Name the program initiated by the city of Cleveland to reclaim its nickname, "Forest City."

S What local heavyweight knocked down Ezzard Charles four times before winning a 10-round decision at the Arena in 1943?

A

AE "Louie, Louie."

B Heinen's.

G North Royalton, at 1,238 feet above sea level, and 375 feet above Lake Erie.

H Clean-Land, Ohio.

S Jimmy Bivins.

AE What was the first play presented by Karamu House featuring an interracial cast ?

B A sleeping momma cat and her kittens were the mascots of what railroad system once based in Cleveland?

G What four-story granite structure, now an administration building, was the original College of Western Reserve University?

H Abram Garfield, son of James A. Garfield, opened a firm here to practice what profession?

S How did the Browns obtain Bernie Kosar?

AE *Cinderella*, in 1917.

B The Chessie System.

G Adelbert Main.

H Architecture.

S The 1985 supplemental draft.

AE Beat generation poet Allen Ginsberg helped raise money for the legal defense of what Cleveland poet indicted by a grand jury in 1966 on charges of obscenity?

B KeyCorp absorbed Society, which bought Ameritrust, which was previously named … what?

G In 1944, what percentage of the nation's population lived within 500 miles of Cleveland?

H Where did the Perry Monument end up after it was moved to make way for the Soldiers and Sailors Monument on Public Square in 1892?

S Who was the starting center for the Cavs' first game in 1970?

AE d. a. levy. (1942–1968)

B Cleveland Trust.

G 50 percent.

H Perrysburg, Ohio.

S Luther Rackley, selected from the Cincinnati Royals in the expansion draft.

Q

AE What presidential assassin purportedly once performed in Cleveland's Academy of Music?

B What legendary Cleveland industrialist was also a U.S. senator and managed the presidential campaigns of William McKinley?

G Name the only new-car dealer in downtown Cleveland.

H Who was the first permanent settler in Bay Village, where a river now flows in his name?

S Who hit his 500th career home run at Cleveland Municipal Stadium on June 17, 1960?

AE John Wilkes Booth.

B Marcus Alonzo Hanna.

G Central Cadillac.

H Joseph Cahoon.

S Ted Williams.

AE Name the writer whose everyday life is the basis for the comic-book drama series, *American Splendor*.

B Lillian Mary Westropp was co-founder of what bank, eventually bought by Charter One in 1992?

G What is the eastern-most stop on RTA's Red Line?

H In 1924, at the request of President Calvin Coolidge, what event was held in Cleveland rather than Chicago?

S What four Indians have won Rookie of the Year honors?

AE Harvey Pekar.

B Women's Federal Savings Bank.

G Windermere Rapid Station in East Cleveland.

H The 1924 Republican National Convention.

S Herb Score (1950), Chris Chambliss (1972), Joe Charboneau (1980), Sandy Alomar (1992).

AE What landscape architect, known for his design of New York City's Central Park, was hired to plan the Cleveland Metroparks "Emerald Necklace"?

B What Cleveland company became one of the country's largest insurance firms by selling high-risk auto policies?

G What church, located in University Circle, is nicknamed "Church of the Holy Oil Can" because of its distinctive Gothic-style spire?

H Around the turn of the century, a confidence artist named Cassie Chadwick tried to secure loans by claiming to be the daughter of what local industrialist and bachelor?

S Why did Jim Brown leave the game of football in 1965?

AE   Frederick Law Olmstead.

B   Progressive Corp.

G   The Epworth-Euclid United Methodist Church.

H   Andrew Carnegie.

S   To pursue an acting career.

AE Don and Marilyn Bianchi, Barry Silverman, and Mark Silverberg founded this Heights-based theater and named it with an acronym based on their own names. What is it called?

B Brothers Joseph, Jack, and Morton Mandel founded what Cleveland distribution company?

G Between 1900 and 1930, the greatest number of Cleveland's immigrants came from what two countries?

H Completed in 1927, the 708-foot Terminal Tower remained the tallest building in the world outside of New York City until what year?

S What number did Browns quarterback Bill Nelson wear in the early 1970s?

AE Dobama.

B Premier Industrial Corp.

G Czechoslovakia and Poland.

H 1967.

S 16.

AE   *Jacobellis v. Ohio* (1964), the landmark decision by the U.S. Supreme Court reaffirming its right to independently determine specific instances of obscenity, emanated from a 1959 showing of the French film *Les Amants* (The Lovers) at what Cleveland movie house?

B   Although he started his career making bicycles, this man is credited with the first sale, in 1898, of an American-made standard-model gasoline automobile, which was manufactured in Cleveland. Who was he?

G   Public Hall and Music Hall are adjacent to which downtown facility?

H   A prominent Cleveland attorney and onetime mayor (1912-16), Newton D. Baker held what position in President Woodrow Wilson's cabinet?

S   What Cleveland high school won the USA Today National Football Championship in 1989 and 1993?

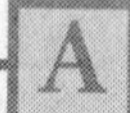

AE The Heights Art Theater in Cleveland Heights (now the Centrum). Owner Nico Jacobellis's conviction on obscenity charges was reversed in the decision.

B Alexander Winton (1860-1932). (The sale came after Winton's famous "Cleveland-New York Drive" in July, 1897).

G The Cleveland Convention Center.

H Secretary of War.

S St. Ignatius High School.

AE In 1955, a 50-cent ticket would get you in to see French Indonesian beauty Sliva and her 12-foot snake at what (now defunct) theater near E. 9th St. and Chester Ave.?

B What Chevrolet dealer sang, then blew a kiss at the end of his TV commercials?

G Ohio's only urban park in the National Park System was established in Dec. 1974. Name it.

H What suburb of Cleveland was given its name by several surveyors and mathematicians in Moses Cleaveland's founding party?

S The Cleveland Barons of the AHL won the league playoff championship eight times, the last one in 1964. What was the name of the championship cup?

AE   The Roxy Theater.

B   C. Miller.

G   The Cuyahoga Valley National Recreation Area.

H   Euclid.

S   The Calder Cup.

AE What comedian was fired from his job as a news director for Channel 3 before heading to Hollywood to appear in the TV series "McHale's Navy"?

B Bearings Inc. is the nation's largest distributor of what product?

G Which hotel is not located downtown: A) The Ritz-Carlton; B) The Marriott; C) Wyndham Hotel; D) Omni International; E) Radisson?

H What Cleveland physician discovered a disease of the pituitary gland that now bears his name?

S What former Cleveland Brown holds the NFL record for the most games played at linebacker?

AE   Tim Conway.

B   Ball bearings.

G   D) The Omni (it's located at the Cleveland Clinic).

H   Dr. Harvey W. Cushing.

S   Clay Matthews, who has played in more than 250 NFL games.

AE What name was given to the group of sailors who were members of Cleveland pianist Evelyn Freeman's 1940s prewar swing band?

B In 1884, what hospital was formed primarily to treat victims of factory accidents in the Cuyahoga Valley industrial area?

G What arcade was once located at the Atrium Office Plaza, 668 Euclid Ave.?

H Trapped in her Statler Hotel room by the great snowstorm of November 1913, what physically challenged American celebrity said, "Few times in my life has it been given me to feel sensations akin to those I've experienced as a captive of the blizzard in Cleveland"?

S Who was the last Cleveland Brown to win the NFL Most Valuable Player Award?

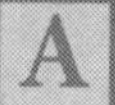

AE   "Gobs of Swing."

B   St. Alexis Hospital.

G   Taylor Arcade.

H   Helen Keller.

S   Brian Sipe, in 1980.

Q

AE What Cleveland DJ was instrumental in bringing Elvis Presley here for his first performance in the North in 1955 and later hosted Elvis's TV debut in New York?

B What research complex, now famous for its holiday light display, was among the first suburban industrial parks developed in the U.S.?

G Which downtown bank lobby, at more than 30 acres, was the largest in the U. S. when it was built in the 1920s?

H In which southwestern suburb of Cleveland did young John D. Rockefeller and his family first live after relocating from New York State?

S Mickey Mantle was the first player to hit a home run out of Cleveland Municipal Stadium. True or false?

AE Bill Randle.

B Nela Park.

G Huntington Bank Building.

H Strongsville.

S False. A ball was never hit out of Cleveland Stadium, nor was one ever hit into the outfield bleachers.

AE What former Warrensville Heights High student was the first black host of a nationally televised late-night talk show?

B Twinsburg-based Universal Electronics Inc. makes what? A) universal remote controls; B) computer software; C) coaxial cable; D) computer chips.

G After Gateway's completion, what new name did the merchants in the area between E. 9th and E. 18th streets, Euclid Ave. and the freeway give their district?

H The Rockefeller Building, at the corner of Superior Ave. and W. 6th St., stands on the former site of what lodging house, which once sheltered President-elect Abraham Lincoln in 1861?

S Who was the last Brown inducted into the Pro Football Hall of Fame?

AE   Arsenio Hall.

B   A) universal remote controls.

G   WelcomeGate.

H   Weddell House.

S   Running back Leroy Kelly, inducted in 1994.

AE What Little Italy school was converted to studio and retail space for artists of varied disciplines?

B Placed on the National Register of Historic Places in 1983, this coral-colored residential complex towers above the Rocky River. Name it.

G Heading towards the lake on the Inner Belt, how many speed grids greet you before Dead Man's Curve?

H This famous Great Lakes steamer sank in November 1975, bound for Cleveland with a load of iron ore. Name it.

S Name the Hall of Fame quarterback who led Cleveland to the NFL Championship in 1945.

A

AE Murray Hill School.

B The Westlake Hotel in Rocky River.

G 10.

H *The Edmund Fitzgerald.*

S Bob Waterfield.

AE Under what pen name did *Cleveland Press* writer Herman Fetzer (1899-1935) write a popular column entitled "Pippins and Cheese," as well as many stories and poems for *The New Yorker*, *Collier's*, and *The Nation*?

B What Lyndhurst-based company built *Pioneer 10*, the first man-made object to leave the solar system?

G Hough Ave. becomes Mt. Sinai Dr. at the intersection of what street?

H The smallest craft ever to sail across the Atlantic Ocean nonstop, used by Robert N. Manry in 1965, is now on display at the Western Reserve Historical Society. Name it.

S Prior to Albert Belle in 1995, who was the last Indian to win the AL home run title?

AE Jake Falstaff.

B TRW.

G Ansel Rd.

H *The Tinkerbelle*.

S Rocky Colavito hit 42 round-trippers in 1959.

AE What famous architect and Cleveland native designed the renovated Cleveland Play House complex (opened in 1983), which houses the Drury, Brooks, and Bolton theaters under one roof?

B What carrier service was the first in Cleveland to start bicycle deliveries in the mid-1980s?

G Which West Side suburb was known as Dover Village until 1940?

H In what year did Western Reserve University and Case Institute of Technology merge to form Case Western Reserve University?

S What future two-time NBA championship coach spent more than 40 games as the Cavs coach during the 1981-82 season?

AE Philip Johnson.

B Quicksilver.

G Westlake.

H 1967.

S Chuck Daly.

Q

AE Which Cleveland Orchestra musical director would not allow musicians to wear beards or mustaches?

B Although machinery lubricants are its main products, what Wickliffe company has also dabbled in vegetable oil?

G What is the name of the City of Cleveland's greenhouse?

H Where did Mayor Michael R. White attend college?

S In 1955-56, three rookies led the Rochester Royals in scoring. The next time this occurred in the NBA was on the 1986-87 Cavaliers team. Who were the rookies?

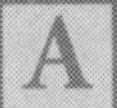

AE George Szell.

B Lubrizol Corp.

G The Rockefeller Park Greenhouse.

H Ohio State University.

S Ron Harper, Brad Daugherty, and John Williams.

AE What 1972 Parma High School graduate portrayed an attorney defending a boy who befriends a gorilla in *Born to Be Wild* and a neurotic psychiatrist in the comic soap opera *Muscle*?

B George M. Humphrey was U.S. secretary of the treasury in the Eisenhower administration and longtime president of what Cleveland company?

G The City of Cleveland has the third largest population among Ohio's cities. True or false?

H In 1867, what happened to force the removal of the fencing that had enclosed all of Public Square since 1857?

S What was the last outdoor professional soccer team to play in Cleveland?

AE Alan Ruck.

B M. A. Hanna Co.

G False. (It is second, after Columbus).

H A court ruled that Superior Ave. and Ontario St. were continuous streets.

S The Cleveland Cobras. The Cobras folded after the 1979 season.

AE What rock group used the Main Street Bridge in Kent on the cover of its first album?

B What local company went public in 1994 with the largest initial public offering in history by a retail chain?

G The Cleveland Play House is one of how many theaters in Playhouse Square?

H Which of the following is not attributable to Eliot Ness while serving as Safety Director from 1935–1942? A) founded police training school; B) instituted radio-dispatched squad cars; C) captured the Torso Murderer; D) started the Cleveland Emergency Patrol.

S Who is credited with christening the bleachers at Cleveland Municipal Stadium "The Dawg Pound"?

AE The James Gang.

B OfficeMax.

G The Cleveland Play House is not part of Playhouse Square.

H C) captured the Torso Murderer.

S Frank Minnifield and Hanford Dixon, during the 1984-85 season.

AE What happened to the tens of thousands of news photos and press clippings from the defunct *Cleveland Press* ?

B What local business award recognizes the fastest-growing businesses in northeast Ohio?

G Although only 10 stories high, this red sandstone structure, built in 1890, was proclaimed to be "Cleveland's first skyscraper." It was placed on the National Register of Historic Places in 1976. Name it.

H What was the irreverent nickname given Mayor Anthony J. Celebrezze, the first Italian-American to reach the office?

S From 1936 to 1969, the Football City Champion was crowned after winning what game held at Cleveland Municipal Stadium on Thanksgiving Day?

AE They were given to the Cleveland State University Archives.

B The "Weatherhead 100."

G The Society for Savings Building on Public Square.

H "The Mustache."

S The Charity Game, played between the East and West Senate Champions.

AE In the 1970s, sculptor Isamu Noguchi was commissioned by the Gund foundation to create what modern piece for the front of the new downtown Justice Center?

B Japan's Kobe Steel Co. bought half of what Lorain steel works in 1989?

G The Hope Memorial Bridge was renamed after comedian Bob Hope, whose father worked as a stone carver on the project. What was the former name of this bridge?

H Although it was one of 100 nationwide job-training programs created by the Economic Opportunity Act of 1964, it had the distinction of producing the first program graduates in the country. Name it.

S What former offensive tackle, who once made 194 consecutive starts for the Browns, later served as the color commentator on Browns game radio telecasts?

AE *Portal.*

B USX Corp.

G Lorain-Carnegie Bridge.

H The Cleveland Job Corps.

S Doug Dieken.

AE What "modern convenience" did The Theatre Comique introduce to the Flats in the mid 1880s?

B Tremco was a longtime Cleveland sealants and coatings maker when it was bought by what Akron company in 1979?

G Alta House, Little Italy's community center, lost its historic main building to a fire in 1981. What is now located on the site of the main building?

H On Feb. 9, 1928, notable Cleveland rabbi Barnett Brickner debated the question "Is Man a Machine?" before a standing-room-only crowd at Public Hall and an estimated 500,000 listeners over radio station WHK. What famous American attorney did he debate?

S What sports legend made his only appearance as a professional golfer at the True Temper Open on Aug 17, 1937 at Acacia Country Club?

AE Gas lighting.

B B.F. Goodrich Co.

G Bocce courts.

H Clarence Darrow.

S Babe Ruth. (His foursome included Tris Speaker, Tommy Armour, and Billy Burke. Ruth did not finish in the money.)

AE   Brutus Thornapple is the main character in what strip created by Lakewood cartoonist Art Sansom in 1965 (and still drawn by Sansom's son, Chip).

B   Built in the early 1960s, what was Ohio's first all-indoor shopping mall?

G   Where is Collision Bend?

H   Founded as the Brooks School for Ladies in 1876, this Shaker Heights school is the oldest surviving private girls' school in Cleveland. Name it.

S   What nickname did the 1980-81 Browns acquire thanks to their habit of winning in the final seconds of a game?

AE "The Born Loser."

B Severance Center in Cleveland Heights.

G On the Cuyahoga River in the Flats.

H Hathaway Brown.

S The Kardiac Kids.

AE Name the Cleveland-raised rock guitarist who used his slide work and power chords as a driving force for the James Gang, the Eagles, and his own solo career.

B This large facility in Brook Park opened as the Cleveland Bomber Plant in November, 1943, and was subsequently known as the Cadillac Tank Plant. By what name is it referred to now?

G Established as the village of Claribel in 1917, this suburb was the last portion of the original Euclid Township to be incorporated as its own village. Name it.

H John Carroll, for whom the university is named, was the first American priest to be elevated to what position?

S During his nine-year career, how many games did Jim Brown miss due to injury?

AE Joe Walsh.

B The I-X Center.

G Richmond Heights.

H Bishop.

S None.

AE Name the Cleveland rock 'n' roll event produced by disc jockey Alan Freed and record retailer Leo Mintz that attracted 25,000 people to the Cleveland Arena in 1952.

B Hugh O'Neil's local cartage firm, founded in 1899 and fully motorized in 1912, is now a major corporation known by what name?

G Is Whiskey Island an island?

H Which Cleveland mayor was forced to call in the Ohio National Guard during the Hough riots in the summer of 1966?

S Who kicked the winning field goal in the overtime victory against the NY Jets during a 1986 playoff game?

AE The "Moon Dog Coronation Ball."

B Leaseway Transportation Corp.

G No. It is a small peninsula bounded by Lake Erie, the Cuyahoga River, and the Old River Bed channel.

H Ralph Locher.

S Mark Mosley.

AE What's the name of the Cleveland ensemble dedicated to 17th- and 18th-century music?

B Name the Cleveland company long considered the creator of sports marketing and management.

G On what floor is the Society Center's observation deck?

H The Pulitzer Prize-winning author of *A Stillness at Appomattox* (1954) broke into journalism with the *Cleveland News* in 1920. Name him.

S Prior to becoming involved in the 1919 Black Sox scandal, this great hitting outfielder spent two years in a Cleveland uniform. What was his name?

AE Apollo's Fire.

B International Management Group.

G The Society Center has no observation deck.

H Bruce Catton (1899-1978).

S "Shoeless" Joe Jackson.

AE What popular TV meteorologist also hosts the annual Woollybear Festival?

B What company still advertises its phone number as "Garfield 1-2323, Garfield 1-2323"?

G On which downtown street will you find the American Red Cross Building?

H How much money did automobile inventor Alexander Winton spend on gasoline for his 47-hour and 34-minute, 707.4-mile excursion from Cleveland to New York, the first long-distance car trip in the U.S.?

S The failed recruitment of which future NBA player landed CSU's basketball team on NCAA probation?

AE Dick Goddard.

B Aluminum Siding Corp.

G Euclid Ave.

H One dollar.

S Manute Bol.

AE Name the two brothers who both anchored local TV newscasts in the 1970s.

B What car accessories company was started with only five dollars in seed money in the 1960s by Cleveland native Joe Hrudka?

G Match the downtown Adult Entertainment venue with its proper address:
a) The Crazy Horse Saloon; b) Circus Circus; c) Tiffany's Cabaret.
1) 1041 Old River Rd.; 2) 1180 Main Ave.; 3) 1438 St. Clair Ave.; 4) I have no idea. I swear.

H Antoinette Brown Blackwell, a member of the Young Ladies' Association of Oberlin College's Institution for the Promotion of Literature and Religion during the 1830s, was the first woman to hold what title?

S What was the first home of the NBA Cleveland Cavaliers?

AE Judd and John Hambrick.

B Mr. Gasket.

G [a-3]; [b-1]; [c-2]

H Minister.

S The Cleveland Arena, at E. 37th and Euclid Ave.

AE The Cleveland Chamber of Commerce paid $10 to buy the first commercially sold image by what famous American photographer, a Cleveland resident at the time?

B What retailer advertises itself as the oldest sporting goods store in Cleveland?

G A WPA enlargement project at this site in 1936 was the biggest in Ohio and moved one million cubic yards of dirt. What facility was enhanced?

H By the 1940s, the numerous structures spanning the Cuyahoga River brought what monicker to the Cleveland area?

S During the 1970s, what individual owned the Indians, the Barons, and the Cavaliers?

AE Margaret Bourke-White.

B Blepp Coombs, at 2020 Euclid Ave.

G Cleveland Municipal Airport. (The enlargement doubled the landing area, making it the largest commercial landing field in the world at that time.)

H "City of Bridges."

S Nick Mileti.

AE What Cleveland newspaper writer could be considered the "Mother of all Rock Critics"?

B What restaurant, opened in Shaker Heights in 1947, was famed for its sauerkraut balls?

G Within 10, what is the number of clear days in a typical Cleveland year?

H What was the nickname of the transit vehicle that carried workers from their homes on Triskett and Berea roads to the Cleveland Bomber Plant during World War II?

S Who was the last Cleveland Indian to win the AL Most Valuable Player Award?

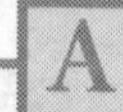

AE *The Plain Dealer*'s Jane Scott.

B Gruber's.

G 66.5 (based on statistics recorded over a 53-year period.)

H "The Bomber Bus."

S Al Rosen, in 1953.

AE In 1949, what famous medical missionary requested to see the Cleveland Museum of Art's McMyler organ during his only visit to the United States?

B What thrift bought Shaker Savings in 1978?

G Brookpark Rd. on Cleveland's West Side has the city's highest concentration of what type of entertainment?

H What was Fred Kohler's most colorful act during his two-year stint (1922-24) as mayor of Cleveland?

S Where did the Cleveland Barons first play when they joined the AHL in 1936?

AE Albert Schweitzer.

B Ohio Savings Association.

G Adult entertainment.

H Having city-owned properties painted orange and black.

S The Elysium Ice Rink, at the corner of Euclid Ave. and E. 107 St.

AE Led Zeppelin's performance at Musicarnival on July 20, 1969 was eclipsed by what historic event?

B Dr. Edwin Beeman was a 19th-century Clevelander known as the "King of …" what?

G This historic neighborhood near E. 55th and Fleet Ave. derives its name from a suburb in Prague. Name it.

H When congressman Chester C. Bolton died in 1939 his wife Frances P. Bolton served out his term, and continued to win re-election in the 22nd district until 1968. Who defeated her, ending the Boltons' 39-year reign in Congress?

S Which late local businessman created a wrestling dynasty at St. Edward High School?

AE   The Apollo 11 moon landing.

B   Chewing gum.

G   Karlin. (It was named by an early Czech settler who opened a saloon and meat market there in 1891.)

H   Charles Vanik.

S   Howard Ferguson.

AE In addition to his famous amateur talent show, this performer also appeared as "Uncle Jake" on a local afternoon television program for children. Who was he?

B What manufacturer, headquartered on St. Clair Ave., is the world's largest supplier of fluorescent pigments?

G In what municipality will one find "Birdtown"?

H Name the second outdoor shopping center in the U.S., built in Cleveland in 1927-29.

S What two brothers graduated from St. Joe's and went on to productive defensive careers in the NFL during the late 1980s?

AE Gene Carroll.

B Day-Glo Color Corp. (owned by RPM).

G Lakewood. ("Birdtown," or "The Bird's Nest," derives its flighty name from these narrow neighborhood streets: Thrush, Lark, Robin, Quail, and Plover.)

H Shaker Square.

S Bob (Patriots, Browns, and Raiders) and Mike Golic (Eagles, Oilers).

AE Why did the Agora close in October 1984?

B What grocery retailer originally operated out of a private home on Hessler Rd. in University Circle in the early 1970s?

G You can still eat at the lunch counter of what old-time dime store located at E. 3rd and Euclid Ave.?

H The Alta House, a settlement house established in 1895 in Little Italy and funded by John D. Rocke-feller, was named for whom?

S Who was the last Indian to win the American League batting crown?

AE It burned down.

B The Food Co-op.

G F. W. Woolworth & Co.

H Alta Rockefeller Prentice, Rockefeller's daughter.

S Bob Avila, who batted .341 in 1954.

AE What Warrensville Heights tent theater, built in 1954, staged summer stock productions such as *The King and I* and *Oklahoma* in the round?

B What caused Mayor Ralph J. Perk's hair to catch on fire as he was opening a national metals organization meeting at Public Hall?

G In what nearby township does the heaviest average rainfall and snowfall for the entire state of Ohio occur?

H What caused the most disastrous fire in Cleveland's history, severely damaging one square mile of the city's East Side and claiming 130 victims?

S What sports facility is known by its advertising slogan, "Every nineteen minutes, the place goes crazy!"?

AE   Musicarnival.

B   Sparks from a welder's torch.

G   Chardon. It averages over 45 inches of rain annually and 106 inches of snow per season.

H   The East Ohio Gas Co. explosion of 1944.

S   Northfield Park harness racing track, opened in 1957.

AE Which former WMMS-FM DJ is included in the "regional listening station" exhibit at the Rock and Roll Hall of Fame and Museum?

B *The Aliened American* was the first newspaper to serve what community in the Cleveland area?

G The Rock and Roll Hall of Fame is located at the site of what harbor?

H During the 1930s, what was the nickname for the Third Precinct area, south of Prospect between E. 55th St. and the Flats, which was full of decaying neighborhoods, gambling joints, bars, and brothels?

S Why were the Indians forced to forfeit a game to the Texas Rangers on June 6, 1974 at Cleveland Municipal Stadium?

AE Kid Leo.

B The African-American community. It ran from 1853 to 1855.

G North Coast Harbor.

H The Roaring Third.

S Drunken fans rushed the field and rioted as a result of the Indians promotion, Dime Beer Night.

AE Which Cleveland Orchestra conductor was called "The Master Builder" for increasing the orchestra's size from 94 to 107 musicians and lengthening the performance season to 49 weeks?

B What was Cleveland Public Power's former name?

G What club occupies a Euclid Ave. mansion that was once home to the General Superintendent of the Western Union Telegraph Co.?

H Warrensville Township, established in 1816, is named after what early settler?

S Name the two Hall of Famers who served as player/coach for the Cleveland Indians World Championship teams in 1920 and 1948, respectively.

AE George Szell.

B The Municipal Electric Light Plant (more popularly known as Muny Light).

G The University Club, at 3813 Euclid.

H Daniel Warren.

S Tris Speaker (1920) and Lou Boudreau (1948).

AE What famous entertainer moved with his family from England to Cleveland in 1907 at the age of four?

B PIANO is an acronym for what area trade group?

G What suburb was formerly known as East Rockport?

H This vessel sank 10 Japanese warships and 30 merchant ships, and damaged 7 others, in addition to rescuing the entire crew of a Dutch submarine, during World War II. Name it.

S What high school senior did the Indians select with their first pick in the 1991 amateur draft?

AE   Bob Hope.

B   Printing Industry Association of Northern Ohio.

G   Lakewood.

H   *The USS Cod*, now moored in North Coast Harbor.

S   Outfielder Manny Ramirez.

AE Name the film that featured scenes filmed at Tremont's St. Theodosius Russian Orthodox Cathedral, Lemko Hall, and LTV's blast furnaces.

B What media conglomerate owned the *Cleveland Press*?

G This park offers seasonal hayrides, thousand-foot toboggan chute runs, and two lakes whose names resemble that of a nearby college. Name it.

H Who is buried in the Garfield Monument?

S Whom did the Indians receive as a result of trading Rocky Colavito to the Detroit Tigers in April of 1960?

AE *The Deer Hunter* (1978).

B Scripps Howard.

G Mill Stream Run Reservation in Strongsville. (Baldwin Lake and Wallace Lake were formed from former rock quarries.)

H President James A. Garfield, his wife Lucretia, his daughter, and her husband.

S Outfielder Harvey Kuehn, the 1959 American League batting champion.

AE This noted stage and screen actor debuted as a "Curtain Puller" at the Cleveland Play House in 1940 under his real name, Joel Katz. Name him.

B What Cleveland-born company developed the "flying printing press," a portable unit for printing multi-color maps, charts, and reconnaissance photos, for the U.S. Army in 1951?

G Five of downtown's busiest streets used to be named for the Great Lakes. Which two names are no longer in existence?

H Where was the original site of the Cleveland Zoo?

S In what league did the Browns play prior to joining the NFL?

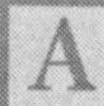

AE Joel Gray.

B The Harris Corp., founded in Cleveland in 1895 as Harris Automatic Press Co.

G Michigan Ave. (closed for the Terminal Tower project in the 1920s) and Erie St., which became E. 9th St. in 1906. Superior Ave., Ontario Ave., and Huron Rd. remain.

H In Wade Park, on the current site of the Cleveland Botanical Gardens.

S The All-American Football Conference (1946–50).

AE The Old Stone Church contains several stained-glass windows designed by what artist?

B The Cleveland Hospital Service Association was the precursor of what health care insurance company?

G What circle is celebrated in the annual "Parade the Circle" festival held each June?

H Winston Churchill, during a visit to Cleveland, proclaimed, "I think that by all odds, *The Plain Dealer* has the best … of any in the world." The best what?

S Name the infamous final play called by the Browns in the 1981 playoff game against the Oakland Raiders.

A

AE Louis Comfort Tiffany.

B Blue Cross & Blue Shield of Ohio.

G University Circle.

H Name.

S Red Right 88.

AE What longtime local morning TV host has traveled to every continent?

B What Cleveland business school, once called Folsom's Mercantile College, changed its name to David N. Myers College in 1995?

G Of downtown's three arcades, which one is four stories high?

H In what decade did Feargus B. Squire reside in Squire's Castle (located in what is now the North Chagrin Reservation of the Cleveland Metroparks)?

S What great heavyweight fighter did Clevelander Jimmy Bivins defeat in a bout at Cleveland Stadium in August of 1945?

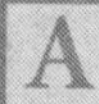

AE Fred Griffin.

B Dyke College.

G The Old Arcade.

H He never lived in the building, which was intended to be the gatehouse for his estate.

S Archie Moore.

Q

AE A 1959 Nash Metropolitan carries what popular TV reporter on his "One Tank Trips"?

B What car dealer ends his politically tinged radio ads by exclaiming, "American, and *proud* of it"?

G The area around E. 105th St. and Euclid Ave., Cleveland's "second downtown" by the 1950s, was also known by what name?

H September 1935 saw the largest crowd ever at Cleveland Municipal Stadium, when approximately 150,000 people gathered for what event?

S Name the two Cleveland attorneys who brought the Davis Cup Challenge Round matches to Cleveland in 1964?

AE Neil Zurcher.

B Bob Serpentini.

G Doan's Corners.

H The Seventh National Eucharistic Congress.

S Harold T. Clark and Bob Malaga.

AE What institution of higher learning, once known as the Western Reserve School of Design, originated in 1882 as a women's art school?

B Cleveland Hopkins Airport serves as a hub for what major airline?

G Name the only Cleveland Metropark not located in Cuyahoga County.

H Home to Cleveland's *fin de siecle* elite, Euclid Ave. was often the scene of what wintertime amateur sport?

S What is the attendance capacity for each of the three ballparks that have been home to the Indians?

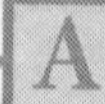

AE   The Cleveland Institute of Art.

B   Continental Airlines.

G   Hinckley Reservation.

H   Sleigh racing.

S   League Park: 22,500; Cleveland Municipal Stadium: 74,483; Jacobs Field: 42,865.

AE What prolific songwriter, who moved from Cleveland to Aliquippa, Pennsylvania as a child, composed "Moon River" and the theme for "Newhart"?

B During World War II, Cleveland Graphite Bronze (later called Clevite) was seized not by the Germans but by a branch of the U.S. armed forces after a strike crippled its production. Which branch?

G Name the Asian retail complex at E. 30th & Payne Ave.

H Before riding into American folklore, John Brown, of Harpers Ferry fame, was raised in what nearby town?

S Which Cleveland team last won a professional championship?

AE Henry Mancini.

B The U.S. Army.

G Asia Plaza.

H Hudson.

S The Cleveland Crunch won the 1995-96 NPSL indoor soccer title.

AE Name the orchestra founded by Cleveland State University professor Edwin London in 1980.

B What building houses much of Greater Cleveland's independent wholesale food industry?

G Greater Cleveland has approximately 5,800 miles of what infrastructure?

H What Cleveland City Council President punctuated an argument with a tossed chair?

S Why did Arena owner Al Sutphin's announcement that he had secured a National Professional Basketball team franchise known as the White Horses surprise most of the city?

AE   Cleveland Chamber Symphony.

B   The Northern Ohio Food Terminal.

G   Water mains.

H   George Forbes.

S   They were expecting a major league hockey team.

AE Cleveland-born record producer and label executive Tommy LiPuma has won six Grammy Awards, including one for his contributions to which Natalie Cole album?

B Although headquartered in Michigan, this company is the largest private-sector employer in Greater Cleveland. Name it.

G On what street and in what suburb did Sam and Marilyn Sheppard live?

H The A. Donald Gray Gardens located behind Cleveland Municipal Stadium are the last remnant of what 1936 event?

S What John Carroll University team achieved its 100th straight Presidents' Athletic Conference victory in 1985?

AE *Unforgettable.*

B Ford Motor Co.

G Lake Rd. in Bay Village.

H The Great Lakes Exposition.

S The wrestling team.

AE What was the price of a lawn seat during Blossom Music Center's first season in 1968?

B What local baking company's "Rock N Roll" rolls helped raise funds for the Rock and Roll Hall of Fame and Museum?

G What is the name of the grassy park at the end of the E. 9th St. pier?

H Name at least three buildings erected as part of the ambitious 1960s urban renewal project called Erieview.

S Who was the last Indians pitcher to win the Cy Young Award?

AE Two dollars. (Pavilion seats were six dollars.)

B Orlando Baking Co.

G Voinovich Park. (Named after George S. Voinovich, mayor of Cleveland 1979-1990.)

H Erieview Tower, One Erieview Plaza, Federal Building, Bond Court Building and Hotel (now Sheraton Centre), Public Utilities Building, and Park Centre.

S Gaylord Perry, in 1972.

Q

AE What prestigious all-male vocal club was founded as a YMCA group in 1893?

B Located at Higbee's on Public Square, this restaurant (closed in 1989) served children's fare in individual drawers of miniature kitchen hutches and was noted for its Art Deco interior design. Name this metallic meal spot.

G The West Side Market has operated at the corner of what two streets since 1912?

H Moses Cleaveland remained in his newly founded colony for approximately how long? A) 2 weeks; B) 3 months; C) 5 years; D) 10 years.

S What organization sponsored track meets at the Arena and the Coliseum for more than 40 years?

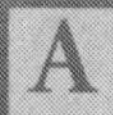

AE The Singers Club of Cleveland.

B The Silver Grille.

G W. 25th and Lorain.

H B) 3 months.

S The Knights of Columbus.

AE Established as the Fairmount Theatre of the Deaf, this performing group has won four local Emmy Awards and two Cleveland Drama Critics' Circle Awards. Name it.

B What cellular phone entrepreneur and future congressman was once arrested at the Galleria for refusing to stop playing a piano on the main floor?

G How many pumping and filtration stations draw water out of Lake Erie for Cuyahoga County?

H What federal judge ordered the desegregation of the Cleveland Public Schools on February 6, 1978?

S Who won the 1974 PGA Championship held at Canterbury Golf Club?

AE Cleveland Signstage Theatre.

B Martin Hoke, U.S. Representative from Ohio's 10th district (Cleveland's West Side).

G Five: Crown, Division, Kirtland, Baldwin, and Nottingham.

H Frank Battisti.

S Jack Nicklaus.

AE What Cleveland Heights amphitheater was constructed with WPA funding in the 1930s?

B What fast food chain was the brainchild of Restaurant Developers Corp.?

G What does it mean if you live "solo" in Ohio City?

H From which bridge did a streetcar plunge on the night of Nov. 16, 1895, killing 17 people?

S Who were the first and second draft choices for the Cavs in 1982 whose last names rhymed?

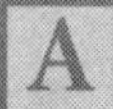

AE Cain Park Theater. (The permanent canopy complex was built in the late 1980s.)

B Mr. Hero.

G You live south of Lorain Rd.

H The Central Viaduct.

S John Bagley, guard, Boston College; Dave Magley, forward, Kansas.

AE Why did the fourth World Series of Rock at Cleveland Stadium start late?

B Which Cleveland taxi service is recognized for being the first to have two-way radio dispatching?

G In the 1930s, what major steel corporation moved its headquarters from Youngstown to Cleveland?

H Name the Cleveland landmark that was torn down for the construction of Jacobs Field and Gund Arena.

S Who was named starting quarterback of the Browns after Bernie Kosar was cut in 1993?

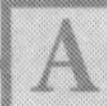

AE   Heavy rains turned the infield into a mud pit.

B   The Yellow Cab Co. (It began installing two-way radios in its cars in Oct. 1944.)

G   Republic Steel.

H   The Central Market (a collection of warehouses and retail establishments bounded by Carnegie Ave., E. 9th St., Ontario Ave. and Huron Rd.).

S   Todd Philcox.

AE Scenes of the Higbee Co. and Public Square were featured in what popular holiday film?

B After leaving Little Tikes in 1989, what second toy company did Thomas Murdough found?

G This Cleveland bridge, the first high-level bridge over the Cuyahoga, featured a lower level for streetcar traffic when it opened in 1917. Name it.

H This Lakewood native served the most consecutive years as Ohio's chief executive. Name him.

S What University of Michigan and St. Joe's wide receiver ran away with the Heisman Trophy voting in 1991?

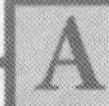

AE *A Christmas Story* (1983).

B Step Two Corp.

G The Veterans Memorial (Detroit-Superior) Bridge.

H Richard F. Celeste, Ohio governor from 1978 to 1990.

S Desmond Howard.

AE The longest-running film in Cleveland history, at more than 20 years, relocated in 1987 from the Heights Art Theater to the Cedar Lee Theater, where it is still shown weekly. Name it.

B A 1974 Forest City Hospital benefit appearance by Muhammad Ali launched the multi-million-dollar career of what sports promoter?

G What's the first bridge across the mouth of the Cuyahoga?

H What was the nickname of Alex Birns, one of Cleveland's most colorful organized crime figures?

S Which Brown leads the team with the most Pro Bowl selections?

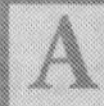

AE The Rocky Horror Picture Show.

B Don King.

G A railroad bridge (Conrail No. 1, nicknamed "The Iron Curtain").

H "Shondor."

S Jim Brown, who was selected each of his nine seasons.

Cleveland Guides & Gifts ...

If you enjoyed this book, you'll want to know about these other fine Cleveland guidebooks and giftbooks ...

Cleveland Ethnic Eats
$12.95 softcover • 208 pages

An insider's guide to 251 *authentic* ethnic restaurants and markets in Greater Cleveland as recommended by the experts: Cleveland's ethnic citizens themselves.

Neil Zurcher's Favorite One Tank Trips
$12.95 softcover • 208 pages

At last! TV's "One Tank Trips" in a book. Ohio's travel expert shows where to take delightful mini-vacations close to home. Hundreds of unusual getaway ideas.

Cleveland Discovery Guide
$12.95 softcover • 208 pages

The best family recreation in Greater Cleveland collected in a handy guidebook. Written by parents, for parents; offers detailed descriptions, suggested ages, prices, & more.

Cleveland Golfer's Bible
$12.95 softcover • 240 pages

Describes in detail every golf course, driving range, and practice facility in Greater Cleveland. Includes descriptions, prices, ratings, locator maps.

Cleveland Garden Handbook
$12.95 softcover • 264 pages

Advice from local experts on how to grow a beautiful lawn and garden in Northeast Ohio. Filled with practical tips and good ideas.

Color Me Cleveland
$4.95 softcover • 32 pages

The All-Cleveland coloring book. Any ages and skill level. Heavy-duty pages.